Believe

A devotion book for those searching for the love of Christ

By
Marian Fryga

Significance of title

When my husband left me on Dec. 27, 2003, I decided one month later in January to try journaling. For years I have taught students to write and encouraged them to journal but I never had. Now I am so thankful God led me to do this. I have reread entries with tears and joy as I recalled painful moments and joy because the journey has led me to a closer walk with God. My first journal was entitled *Believe*. The original meaning was I believed in a miracle that my marriage could be saved. I prayed for that. As time went on I changed my prayers to "God your will be done." As months passed God, the God of all truth, revealed many truths about my ex and myself. My prayers changed to "God please don't send him back and don't reveal any more truths." *Believe?* I believe in God the father, the maker of heaven and earth and how that same creator can make changes for your life for the better. The word "believe" appears in the book of John 27 times. That makes you think doesn't it? If we understood the importance of this one word our lives would change. John 7:38 "Whoever believes in me, as the Scripture has said, streams of living water will flow from within him." Tap in to this source of strength in Christ and allow streams of living water nourish you constantly. John 20:27 "Stop doubting and believe." Believe God can make a difference in your life and in the lives of those whom you love. My prayer is that through this book you might see the changes God has made in me and find hope and encouragement for your own walk with Christ.

Make this your prayer. Insert your name on the blanks. Mark 9:22-24 "But if you can do anything, take pity on _____and help _____. If you can? Said Jesus, "Everything is possible for him who **believes.**" Immediately the boy's father (you) exclaimed, _____does believe; help me overcome my unbelief!"

Foreword

Writing this devotion book is a maturation process in itself. It is taking me back to places of hurt I had forgotten or categorized in a box to not open again until later. This is the later "for such a time as this" Esther 4:14. It is worth it all if it will help someone else make it through a tough time. Matthew 16:24-25 "Then Jesus said to his disciples 'If anyone would come after me, he must deny himself and take up his cross and follow me." I pray, Lord, that you will help me to deny myself so that I may carry your cross. Use these devotions and diary entries of mine to your glory. Lord, I will deny myself to follow you. You know what is on my heart and I desire that. Amen.

> How beautiful on the mountains
> Are the feet of those who bring good news,
> Who proclaim peace,
> Who bring good tidings,
> Who proclaim salvation,
> Who say to Zion,
> "Your God reigns!"
> Listen! Your watchmen lift up their voices;
> Together they shout for joy.
> When the Lord returns to Zion,
> They will see it with their own eyes.
> Burst into songs of joy together,
> You ruins of Jerusalem.
> For the Lord has comforted his people,
> He has redeemed Jerusalem.
> The Lord will lay bare his holy arm
> In the sight of all the nations,
> And all the ends of the earth will see
> The salvation of our God.
>
> Depart, depart, go out from there!
> Touch no unclean thing!
> Come out from it and be pure,
> You who carry the vessels of the Lord.
> But you will not leave in haste
> Or go in flight;
> For the Lord will go before you,
> The God of Israel will be your rear guard.
> Isaiah 52:7-12

Journals

Journal Feb. 4, 2004 6:35 AM
I called two of my prayer warrior friends first thing this morning. One said Job was tested until he told God you can kill me but I will still trust in you and when you do I'll just be with you in a better world. That is faith! Even though Satan has thrown me some curves with our money and the questions I have about what is happening with it I still believe this marriage can work. God can call my husband to him. I am inspired to read about the miracles in the Bible now because I do BELIEVE in miracles. My other friend told me to read Psalm 91 and pray for my children and husband each one at a time as I pray aloud the Psalm. I just did that. I especially liked Psalm 91 verses 9-12 "If you make the Most High your dwelling-even the Lord, who is my refuge- then no harm will befall you, no disaster will come near your tent, For he will command his angels concerning you to guard you in all your ways; they will lift you up in their hands, so that you will not strike your foot against a stone."

Journal Feb. 6, 2004 4:00 AM
I can't sleep. I woke up at about 3 and it is now 4. I reread two chapters in a Purpose Driven Life. Chap. 16 "What Matters Most" on love and Chap. 14 "When God Seems Distant." I need God's love now more than ever. I want to resolve to pray daily the prayer on p. 126 "God, whether I get anything else done today, I want to make sure that I spend time loving you and loving other people-because that's what life is all about. I don't want to waste this day."

Journal Feb. 7, 2004 6:30 AM
Philippians 2:12-13 "Therefore, my dear friends, as you have always obeyed –not only in my presence, but now much more in my absence- continue to work out your salvation with fear and trembling, for it is God who works in you to will and to act according to his good purpose." The way this relates to me recently is I feel like I have always obeyed Christ before this separation occurred, but I have also continued to trust in the Lord even in His absence. I feel at times like He has abandoned me during this difficult time in my life. I have cried out to God. I have rejoiced in God. I have questioned God. I have tried to focus on others rather than myself. The fear and trembling only relates to my fear of the future and whether I can do this. I am so full of love, yet God is taking away (or Satan) the one person on earth I love most. I fear and tremble about the future, yet I trust in God. "For it is God who is working in me" and I believe He is leading me to act in his good purpose. I have been trying to do that "act in his good purpose."

Journal Feb. 7 7:30 PM
It occurred to me tonight that taking my husband back after the first
affair –this was my thanks-leaving me. That is one bitter thought and I
should never have thought of that. I am sure Satan put that thought into
my head. Anger sets in at times about this whole thing. Having him here
on the weekends is difficult. Having him around makes me miss him
more. In a relationship with Christ how does Christ deal with loss? His
capacity to love is far greater than mine. It hurts so much. Why this is
necessary I don't know.

Feb. 8 7:30 AM
I want to journal on why suffering is necessary. It is necessary to suffer for
growth. I need to have patience to trust God that through all of this
suffering it will lead to a good end. I am not sure what that good end will
be but He is taking me there. My future may or may not include my
husband. I don't know. All I can do at this point is wait for the Lord to take
his action with him and I will be there for whatever the result may be.
Romans 5:3-5 … "but we also rejoice in our sufferings, because we know
that suffering produces perseverance; perseverance character; and
character, hope. And hope does not disappoint us, because God has poured
out his love into our hearts by the Holy spirit." Last night after my husband
left I cried uncontrollably, sobbing. I called my sister. She advised me to
avoid my husband today at church. I told her that wasn't the answer. She
was just looking for a way to help me heal my hurt. Running from my
problems is not going to be a way to deal with it. I must face my problems
head on. Jesus is the best example of facing suffering. When I think of
Christ who am I to think I am suffering? The assurance comes from the
fact that I know Jesus shares my emotions, hurts, and feelings. He relates
to my every tear. He hurts when I hurt. He is at peace when I am at peace.
This feeling of peace within is what has kept me going through all of this.
That sense of peace is God's Spirit within me. There is a wholeness about
it, an indescribable joy. Thank you, Lord, for loving me that much!

Feb. 16 2:00 PM
At church an impending doom came over me. My husband was talking
excitedly about bad weather coming mid afternoon like he was anxious
not to spend the whole afternoon at the house. He said we should get our
son to head back to Charleston early. I felt like he would be anxious to
leave as well. I felt at the bottom of lows and questioned God about how
I could even be feeling that way while I sat in church. I could sense that
the friends who sit behind us saw my depression. I could not make
myself put on a front of pleasantness. I secretly took off my wedding ring
and put it in my wallet. I felt this was the sign that my husband wasn't
even trying to be with me that afternoon and that he did not want to be
back with me.

Journal Feb. 25 6:05 AM

It has been a long time since I journaled. Many things have happened: anger, disappointment, chastising, blessings, closed doors, God's presence revealed to me, friends of support, and most importantly an inner peace which God gives me.

Journal Feb. 25 2:00 PM

I want to respond to this passage of scripture I read this morning. 2 Corinthians 12:9-10 "My grace is sufficient for you, for my power is made perfect in weakness. Therefore I will boast all the more gladly about my weaknesses, so that Christ's power may rest on me. That is why, for Christ's Sake, I delight in weaknesses, in insults, in hardships, in persecutions, in difficulties. For when I am weak, then I am strong." I think God makes us strong through our weaknesses. God has definitely show me my weaknesses lately and certainly my sons have too. God is here for me during all of my weaknesses. Christ's power is on me. I can feel his presence every day when I trust Him and I don't worry. He is looking after my future. The positives during hardship is growth and there was plenty of room for growth in me. I am so happy to be going to church now when I want to. I held back from going because of my spouse at times. I have never studied the Bible and other inspirational books like I do now. I sleep with the cross I bought on the mission trip under my pillow. I wake up and hold it at night.

Journal Feb. 27 9:30 AM

Paul says in 2 Corinthians "our light and momentary troubles" when he was 1. imprisoned 2. beaten with a whip 5 times 3. faced death 4. beaten with rods three times 5. stoned once 6. shipwrecked three times 7. stranded in the open sea 8. left homeless and 9. hungry and thirsty.

Lord, stop my whining about my situation. Paul made it because he could see "an eternal glory that far outweighs them all." I pray that I focus on that eternal glory. You have so much in store for me yet. You are with me now every step of the way. Praise be to God! God never said that the journey would be easy but he did say the arrival would be worthwhile. Carry me forward into your plan, Lord. Amen.

Feb. 27 snow day 10:00 AM

I read Matthew Chapter 14. The two parts which really struck me 1. were where Jesus found out about John the Baptist being beheaded and he went off privately in a boat to mourn John's loss. But then Jesus landed, saw a large crowd, took compassion on them and healed the sick. All I could think about was how Jesus really wanted time to be alone to mourn, remember, praise his friend's life, remember his baptism and what role John's life had in preparing the way for Him. Even when John was in his mother's womb the baby leapt for joy because of Mary's news of the coming Christ. That is true friendship. John believed without seeing Jesus and then they became friends. No one knew Jesus any better than John the Baptist I would say. I can only imagine how deeply touched Jesus was by John's senseless death – the whim of a young girl on her birthday asking for John's head on a platter. Satan. Despite all these feelings and emotions what really impressed me was Jesus put his self aside and looked to the needs of others. When he saw the large crowd he put his human side aside and selected his Godly side to take compassion to heal the sick. What about the compassion for Jesus? Who was showing Him compassion? His unselfish devotion to others has really touched me. Thank you for that focus in life and your example of how I am to be. Even in a time of trouble I am not to look at myself but turn to others who need me or do something to help others.   2. The passage about Peter and Jesus during the storm really struck me as well. The disciples thought Jesus was a ghost. (Am I like that crying out in fear, elusiveness of a ghost, not real, not trusting during fear that Jesus is real?) Jesus said, "Take courage! It is I! Don't be afraid." Peter said, "If it is you tell me to come to you on the water." Peter got out of the boat walked on the water and came toward Jesus. But when he saw the wind he was afraid and beginning to sink he cried Lord save me! Immediately Jesus reached out his hand and caught him. "You of little faith why did you doubt?" The reason this passage struck me is because I am Peter. I walk out onto the water to Jesus but then I doubt when the winds come. This is my life right now. Why do I doubt? "Trust in the Lord with all your heart, mind, soul, and strength."   "I can do all things through God who strengthens me." "For I know the plans I have for you declared the Lord, plans to prosper you and not to harm you, plans to give you hope and a future." "When I am afraid I will trust in you." "Let the beloved of the Lord rest secure in him , for he shields him all day long, and the one the Lord loves rests between his shoulders." "Be strong and courageous. Do not be terrified; do not be discouraged, for the Lord your God will be with you wherever you go."

Feb. 27 9:00 PM

Let God Surprise You by Heather Macallum and Angela Hunt. "Our God is a God of healing. Sometimes he heals through miracles, sometimes he heals through medicine and sometimes he heals through both. Let God surprise you- pray for guidance, then walk through the doors he opens for you." I have placed this marriage, my sons, and my life in His hands. I want what is best for my children and for me. I want us to find this best through our following God's purpose for us. I am not praying now for our marriage I am praying for God to open the doors for what He wants me to do. I take the selfishness out of this and turn to God to meet my needs as I serve Him, Open the doors of opportunity for me to grow closer to God and do His will. I think I needed to adjust my plan of action from my husband and me to both of my sons and God's plan for me to minister to others. Even Jesus prayed for God to spare him. Don't spare me, Lord, send me on to fulfill my purpose as you sent Jesus on to die for our sins. Thank you, Lord!

Feb. 28 7:00 AM

Lord, I am confused and hurt by why I should have to give up the man I love as my husband. This just doesn't make sense that he could love someone more than me. If I knew what was wrong with our relationship I would fix my side of it. The problem is
he has to want it too and he doesn't. Everything I call him to do to bring us closer to God he pulls away. I have set 2 counseling appointments and he canceled them both. I asked him to attend The Purpose Driven Life class with me and he didn't. I would love to be a tool of reconciliation in this marriage. If I cannot be used to benefit my own marriage then use my life to benefit others in some way.

Feb. 29 5:15 AM

I sure do miss him Lord. I sure do miss him. I looked at my pictures on my bedside table and stared at the handsome man I married. Where is he in there? The man I gave my vows to, the vows we made before God, both of our fathers who married us are both deceased now, and the friends and loved ones in that church. It hurts I miss him so much.

March 2, 2004 3:30 AM

Philippians 3:7-11 "Whatever was to my profit I now consider loss for the sake of Christ." I am willing to lose it all if necessary to make sure I am right with Christ so that I may "love the Lord with all my heart, all my soul and all my mind." He is calling me to do that now. I may have to sacrifice my husband and my boys' love temporarily to achieve that goal. I pray not. "everything is a loss compared to the surpassing greatness of knowing Christ Jesus , my Lord, for whose sake I have lost all things," … "not having a righteousness of my own that comes form the law, but that which is through faith in Christ." I am thinking of the law of marriage, but I must follow through with my complete faith in Christ. If I trust in Him completely He will work this out, not me. I must surrender it all to Him. "I want to know Christ and the power of his resurrection becoming like him in his death …. And to attain resurrection from the dead." I believe this suffering must occur to be Christlike. Suffering is necessary to bring me to my senses. I have attended church all of these years, but I have not truly TRUSTED God with my life. He has me to that point and He is beginning to resurrect me. I am not there yet; I am striving to be resurrected. I am striving to be resurrected. I am a sinner with pride and arrogance. God knows my faults and what has kept me from this "faith in Christ" with my total being and all of my life. I can't worry about my boys' relationship or with my relationship with my husband. I give it all to Christ to handle. I must have MY life right first in order for the other relationships in my life to be right. Resurrect me from the dead, Lord! You have the power to make me yours. You are the potter, I am the clay. Mold me and make me after thy will, while I am waiting, yielded and still. Have thine own way, Lord.

March 5, 2004 4:00 PM

1 Corinthians 12:24-26 "But God has combined the members of the body and has given greater honor to the parts that lacked it, so that there should be no division in the body, but that its parts should have equal concern for each other. If one part suffers, every part suffers with it, if one part is honored, every part rejoices with it." I feel like this as a part of the church community and beyond that to Christian friends. We are a body and they suffer along with me.

Last night I felt a real sense of peace because when I came home my youngest son was here. We had had a hard time this week because he lashed out at me about this separation. He yelled and cussed at me on Wednesday. Thursday I called him and still got a cold shoulder, but he was fine last night. Thank you, Lord, for that blessing. I was so relieved that he wanted to talk about things and I so badly wanted to listen. He talked about work some and the TV show we were watching. We stayed up until after midnight. Thank you, for that time with my son. I went outside. It was 12 pm now but I went down to the dock and sat under the most beautiful sky. White, puffy clouds were flying across the sky covering the full moon and then revealing the moon with open holes in the clouds but never completely hiding it. It felt like a warm spring breeze. I felt the presence of God and heaven. It was as if I felt the saints in heaven looking down on me. God sends me such peace and comfort 24-7. I have found this peace in so many places and ways. I never want to live without this sense of peace again.

March 9 12:30 PM

This morning at the school teacher devotional a friend said what an inspiration I was being to others through how I am handling this situation. Thank you, Lord, for that. I humbly accept this as your will being done through me. If any of what I am going through can benefit someone else I am all for it. You suffered so much for us. The one thing I am concerned about is my selflessness. I pray I do not want this marriage to work for my benefit. I am lonely. I do want companionship. I need to have someone to love and to love me in return. I will continue to pray for my husband, but I have completely turned him over to Christ. My friend said they are praying for him too but that they want me to look after myself. God is looking after myself. I want to become more Christlike every day-focus on others, not myself. Christ did not try to please himself.

April 8 visiting friend's beach house. First Spring break alone.
I am at the beach house. I have changed so much in that I enjoy being alone sometimes and I am not scared to be alone. My friend was worried about me over here alone at the beach house. I am fine. I went on the deck on the marsh side and lay in the hammock. It was a peaceful, beautiful, quiet time with God. I saw three falling stars. I thought about my wishes I used to make on the stars. I used to wish for a horse-I got that and it was a disappointment. I used to wish to marry my husband and that was a disappointment too. I saw the 4th falling star when I went out front on the beach side after I read the Bible some. I wished on this star for spending more time with Christ. That is one wish I know won't be disappointing. When I walked out front on the beach side and saw the beauty of God's creation it took my breath away. I fell to my knees on the boardwalk and thanked God for his blessings to me this day through family, friends, and His creation. The full moon was shining on the ocean Right at the end of the boardwalk. I will try to do it justice by describing the beauty of it. The white reflection shone across the ocean through the calm and onto the sand. The moon was huge and bright. The waves I tried to pick one and watch from way out until it broke close to shore but I could not follow the same one. The waves turned black as they crested into a wall of water and then broke into smaller waves as they approached the shore. Right after the wave broke the water in front of it would go completely calm as it dissipated at the shallow shore. The foam along the edge of the beach was so white! I was mesmerized by it all and the wonder of the tides. Below the moon a reverse night effect of the moonbeams as the sun creates a triangle of light down the moon had a triangle of black immediately under it where its light did not shine. Clouds would come over and cover the moon in thin veils and then glide away. I must have spent an hour out there meditating until midnight. It was so beautiful! Thank you, Lord, for a PERFECT DAY!!

April 9 9:00 AM
The sin I need help with, Lord, is bitterness and resentment. I look back on many aspects of our marriage and I realize the number of times my husband has lied to me. I also realize how selfish he always was. Most of what he did was motivated for himself and what he wanted. God, you are going to have to help me with overcoming the anger and regret I feel over these situations. It is sinful for me to recall incidents daily. Cleanse my spirit. Pour your blood of righteousness and forgiveness on me so that I might forgive him and cause me not to be so judgmental of him. I am just as much a sinner and I pray for your redeeming love in my love for others.   FORGIVE AND FORGET!

April 9 5:30 PM
Isaiah 43:18-19 "Forget the former things; do not dwell on the past. See, I am doing a new thing! Now it springs up; do you not perceive it? I am making a way in the desert and streams in the wasteland." God spoke to me through this passage to give up my past and not dwell on it. What is done is done and I must move on. I should not remember the hurts from the past my husband has caused. Dwelling on the negatives will only bring me down. My best friend said, "Marian, you can grab on to him and drown with him, or you can swim your way out, up, and away to save yourself." I choose to allow God to save me. He is making a way in the desert (difficult times) for me. He will create streams (nourishment, provision) for me even in a wasteland. My marriage these past six years has been a wasteland. Thank you, Lord, for delivering me from it. It was interesting for my oldest son to note these past two years were dragging me down in my relationship with his brother and him. I am definitely refocused on my priorities. God 1st, God leading my every step, and my love for my boys.

April 11 3:00 PM
Psalm 126:4-6 "Restore our fortunes, O Lord, like steams in the Negev. Those who sow in tears will reap with songs of joy. He who goes out weeping, carrying seeds to sow, will return with songs of joy, carrying sheaves with him."This passage speaks to me about my current situation. Even though is has been difficult I feel very positive and optimistic about my future. I am feeling strongly today that God is restoring my fortune in a way I cannot imagine- without my husband. I think he has chosen a life of lying and deceit. I have certainly wept, but I have carried seeds to sow in that I am learning new ways to witness through visiting shutins, opening the gym for the Children's Shelter, helping with FCA, attending Bible studies, and giving money to those who need it. Another important beginning ministry for me is the ministry of prayer. I feel the songs of joy and the sheaves are the bountiful harvests of blessings God sends to me. I love being a servant for Christ and serving others.

April 13 5:30 AM
We must trust God to remove the stone in our lives so that we can see the resurrected Lazarus even though he had been dead four days. What stone is Jesus commanding me to remove so He can set free form sin and spiritual death- my child, my husband? Jesus said to me "If you want to see me work in the life of your Lazarus, take away the stone." God, I don't know if you are still calling to me to remove the stone for my husband. I am healing now and forging ahead for a life without him. Selling this house, running my own finances, getting us out of some of the financial mess we are in, setting my hopes on a future with YOU! I can't do this alone. My husband is making no effort and it has been that way for years. What I do trust, Lord, is turning him over to you. What will come of that I know not, but it will be for his best. John 11:46 "Did I not tell you that if you believed, you would see the glory of God."

Journal April 18, 2004

Today is Sunday. Friday night I prayed that God would reveal an important message to me through His word. On Saturday morning after my devotional a good friend of mine called and told me God told her to tell me these passages to read in the Bible. (That sent chills over my body.) Joshua 1:5, Psalm 32:8, Isaiah 46:4, Isaiah 41:10, Isaiah 49:16, Genesis 28:15,Leviticus 26:12. All of these verses are so reassuring. God sends His love to me!

April 25 7:30 AM

"Blessed are those who hunger and thirst for righteousness, for they shall be filled." Matt. 5:6   I memorized this passage of scripture yesterday. Certain words caught my interest. Last fall I was inspired by God to teach a Sunday school lesson on *thirsty*. He gave me the ideas I needed to teach. The other words which drew my attention are righteousness and filled. I used the dictionary last night to look them both up. Righteousness-1.acting in a just, upright manner; doing what is right 2.morally right; fair and just, moral
Fill-1.n. all that is needed to make full. 2. to make complete by inserting or supplying something. 5. to supply the things needed or called for to satisfy a need, requirement 7. to satisfy the hunger or desire for; feed or satiate.

I do hunger and thirst for everything pertaining to God. This is the assurance he will see me through.

This is the first month, May, that I have been given an alimony payment. God is leading me to tithe 10% even though it was not budgeted by my lawyer. Several things have come up-lawn mower broke, sprinkler system not working, birthdays. This morning I am going to pray for God to Psalm 91 "If you make the most High your dwelling-even the Lord, who is my refuge then no harm will befall you, no disaster will come near your tent. For he will command his angels concerning you to guard you in all your ways; they will lift you up in their hands, so that you will not strike your foot against a stone." I cried this morning for worrying about the finances. I called Mother and she prayed with me, encouraged me, and promised to send me a little money. I love her so much! This is the last aspect of my life I think I have to turn over to God. He will see me through.

April 25 1:00 PM

It was a great day at church. My sons came to church. The sermon today was great! My minister preached on restoring relationships based on Jesus and Peter after Peter had denied Jesus three times. Jesus commissioned Peter to serve the people after he asked him three times, "Do you love me?" I took some notes based on my pastor's admonition to follow Jesus by example. 1. Don't point out mistakes or lecture 2. Have faith in the other 3. Go to Christ with the mistake 4. feel the mistake in my heart 5. Condition of the heart God will know 6. Don't worry about the words when I ask God for forgiveness 7. Jesus affirmed Peter 3 times.   GOD IS IN THE BUSINESS OF RESTORING RELATIONSHIPS.   I cried during the closing hymn. I could tell it touched my oldest son, too. I am sure my youngest son listened today. This was a special time with my family.

What I don't know is if God was sending me a message to have faith in relationships being restored like my husband and me or whether these are just guidelines to use in the future for other new relationships he is going to send me. I'll continue to pray for guidance.

Lord, I don't want to continue in a sense of false hope for my marriage. There is no indication from my husband that he wants our marriage to work at all. He spends less and less time with the boys and he draws farther and farther away from you. Last night he even came in , got more of his things to take with him, and left. I am healing. Thank you, Lord. It is just difficult to see him or even talk to him. You will take care of me through all of this. Thank you for that assurance that you are with me. Amen.

April 25 10:10 PM

Peter walked with Jesus. John 21:21 and glanced back and saw John following them. He must have wondered if living for Jesus was going to be as costly for John as it was for him. "Lord, what about him?" Jesus bluntly responds, "How I work in other people's lives and how they respond to me is basically none of your business." I wanted to write about this because I am afraid I have been doing this with my ex. It is none of my business how God is going to deal with him. I should get the log out of my own eye before I start placing blame on him. My relationship with Christ is **my** business and if I get all things right with Him then my relationships will fall into place with whomever that is supposed to be- my ex, my sons, my mother, my friends. Thank you, Lord, for showing me that. I am to judge only myself not others.

May 2 1:30 PM

Yesterday was a mixed day of emotions. Some college friends called me trying to get in touch with my husband. They were so shocked to know my husband and I had been separated since December. I am amazed at myself that I waited this long to talk with my college friends about it. We all feel a certain closeness because of the significant other we met at college and then married. My ex told me this past fall how much he disliked his college years. That really hurt me because that was when he met me. I never really saw much in him that appreciated any of our memories. He never reflected on being glad he met me. I had just said in October how glad I was that I was married to the man I loved and not wishing I was married to someone else. Isn't that ironic since that was the way he was feeling- wishing he was married to someone else? While I was on the phone the boys were outside screaming and yelling at each other. I didn't like the language they were using so I came back inside since my presence made no discernable difference.I prayed and got a sense of peace over me. I was praying that the boys would get that sense of peace too. Later that evening they were back to normal. I was glad of that. I called their dad right after the boys' argument and gave him a piece of my mind. I felt so much better after having done it too. His selfishness keeps him happy. I guess that is all that matters to him.

May 7 12:00

Lord, don't allow me to become bitter towards my husband. It would certainly help if he could be honest with me about why he left. I think there are a lot of untold things I don't know. Honesty would help the boys cope with this as well. He denies any connection with the other woman. The Bible says "Blessed are the merciful, for they shall obtain mercy." Matthew 5:7 I forgive her. I pray for God to lead her and lead her away from my family. My husband has this loyalty to her I cannot understand. He made vows with me in front of God. I never would have thought commitment meant so little to him. I always respected him for standing for what was right. I guess I misjudged his character. I pray that my bitterness and unforgiveness not become a wall between God and me. This will hinder my prayers if I let this happen. If you forgave all on the cross then surely I can forgive him. Please forgive me, dear Lord. Help me to forgive him. …. I forgive him and I mean it.

May 11 8:50

"Rebuke a discerning man and he will gain knowledge." A friend of mine listens carefully to what I say and then sometimes admonishes me or rebukes me for my actions. I know that she always speaks the truth from her heart. I have committed sins in my relationships with my sons in many ways because they are hurting very much. Selfishness is the one my oldest son stated I did. I pray, Lord, for you to forgive me of any sins I have done out of commission or omission. Improve my relationship with you first so that I may improve my relationship with my sons. I need them very much at this point in my life. Thank you for the sense of peace this morning that everything will be okay. I love you and trust you with my life. Grant me knowledge and discernment so that I may be more Christlike.

"It is to a man's honor or to avoid strife, but every fool is quick to quarrel." Prov. 20:3

"Make plans by seeking advice if you wage war, obtain guidance."Prov.20:18

"Blows and wounds cleanse away evil, and beatings purge the inmost being." Proverbs 20:30

Perhaps what my oldest son and I went through with the arguing this weekend was necessary. I want my inmost being purged. I am encouraged through God's word that our argument was necessary and now we may both move on. This could be part of our healing process. I know it hasn't lessened my love for my son in any way. I respect him for speaking out his mind.

May 15 9:00 AM

I am reading in a Bible study guide. The scripture is James 1:1 through 2:20 on a topic of "How to Make up Your Mind". This is very appropriate for me right now as I decide what to do with selling the house, where to go, whether to buy myself a place, rent from a friend, my relationship with the boys, retirement buying into the TERI program, and what purpose I am to live for Christ. I have a lot of major decisions to make right now. I am excited about 1 Corinthians 2:16 "For who has known the mind of the Lord that he may instruct him? But we have the mind of Christ." What this says to me is the power of the Holy Spirit in me will lead me to make wise choices financially, spiritually, relationally, and otherwise. This is such a relief to know that God will be there to teach me what to do. It is such a relief to know He leads me. It is like having a parent sharing wisdom with me about what decisions to make. All I have to do is trust Him. I am reminded of the hymn God first put on my mind when I was running one day a few days after my husband left-"Trust and Obey, for there's no other way, to be happy in Jesus but to Trust and Obey." That has been my theme and that is what I'll do. The happiness I feel right now and the overwhelming sense of relief is hard to put into words. Thank you, Lord! Thank you, Lord! (The Bible study was Rick Warren's *Developing a Faith that Works vol.1)*

May 18 6:00 AM

In my Bible study this morning Psalms is speaking to me. Psalm 111:10 "The fear of the Lord is the beginning of wisdom." I have been seeking God's wisdom lately. Psalm 104:27 "They all wait for thee. To give them their food in due season." I have been waiting for God to feed me spiritually. He will give me my food in due season. He knows when the timing is right for me. Psalm 145:16 "Thou dost open they hand. And dost satisfy the desire of every living thing." It is so reassuring that God will satisfy my desires. I can see that at work in my life now. He takes care of me down to the minutest detail. Yesterday the power bill for the month was forty dollars less than even last month's low bill. God wants me to tithe and live comfortably. Praise God for his blessings on me.

May 28 8:00 AM

All I get from this morning's Bible study is a message of hope and assurance. 2 Corinthians 6:2 "In the time of my favor I heard you, and in the day of salvation I helped you. I tell you now is the time of God's favor, now is the day of salvation." Isaiah 49:23 "Then you will know that I am the Lord, those who hope in me will not be disappointed." Also my devotion scripture this morning was John 10:10 "I have come in order that you might have life-life in all its fullness." How much more reassuring could that be? I am experiencing happiness right now that I have not felt in a <u>long</u> time. Happiness that comes from studying God's word, having meditation time, and just purely enjoying living. I find pleasure in the smallest things in life now. Last night being on the water in the boat was so much fun. My brother came with his children. They rode on the tube. They had a ball! They enjoyed watching me ski and a friend barefoot. It is fun to have fun again! "I tell you now is the time of God's favor." Thank you, Lord, for all the blessings you share with me.

May 30 7:00 PM

The message I got from today's devotional was pretty obvious to me in my situation regarding last night. Sometimes loneliness hits like a bludgeon. My neighbors were having a supper. My oldest son and I were out on the lake having a ball skiing until dark. He surfed behind the boat. I trick skied. We did just about everything. We went back up to the house and he left to go visit his dad. My youngest son had gone out on a date. I didn't want to be alone so I went over to the next door neighbor's house for their outdoor party. I enjoyed visiting. It got to be 10:30 and I left to go back home to this dark, lonely house by myself. I stayed up and cooked some because cooking makes me happy. I went to bed and tried to sleep but couldn't. I just wanted so desperately to have someone to talk to or someone just to hold me.I got up and went to a guy friend's house to ask him if he would come sit outside and talk with me. It was a little after midnight. I stood there and thought twice about it with my finger on the doorbell. I didn't ring it. I was soooo lonely it hurt. I didn't ring it and went back home. I was so happy God didn't let me do that. I went back to bed and was able to sleep the rest of the night. When I got up this morning the scripture was Acts1:4 "While staying with the apostles, Jesus ordered them not to leave Jerusalem, but to wait there for the promise of the Father." What is said to me was to be patient and wait for God's promise in my life. I think that promise is if I am patient and try to do what is right God will bless my future. I see evidence of that all ready. I can't remember when I have been so happy. So many things in my everyday life make me happy now. I smile so much more. Thank you, Jesus! Waiting upon God is not resignation; it is expectation!

May 31 8:30 AM

In my <u>Upper Room</u> devotion "When we let go of what we think is rightfully ours, we are free to receive the greater good that God offers." I hear God loud and clear on this one. I am giving up my husband, my house, possibly my possessions and sometimes it has felt like my boys. Tithing 10% of what I didn't think I had has been a leap of faith. All of this is trusting God with my life. Right now we are getting much needed rain and I can still see the brightness and glow of the sun through the clouds. I am happy, Lord. I have been praying for wisdom and I feel you have been sharing wisdom with me. I am able to make it financially because of your blessings. I feel like my relationship with my sons is improving. I turn it all over to you, Lord. I turn <u>ALL</u> of my life over to you!

June 1 9:30 AM

2 Corinthians 1:3-7 "Praise be to the God and Father of our Lord Jesus Christ, the Father of compassion and the God of all comfort, who comforts us in all our troubles, so that we can comfort those in any trouble with the comfort we ourselves have received from God. For just as the sufferings of Christ flow over into our lives, so also through Christ our comfort overflows. If we are distressed, it is for your comfort and salvation; if we are comforted, it is for your comfort, which produces in you patient endurance of the same sufferings we suffer. And our hope for you is firm, because we know that just as you share in our sufferings, so also you share in our comfort." This speaks volumes to me this morning. I remember my oldest son saying recently, "Mama, you should consider yourself complimented because Christ chose you to go through this suffering to become more Christlike." I did not know the depth of his faith until then. He is exactly right as the apostle Paul said, "just as the sufferings of Christ flow over into our lives, so also through Christ our comfort overflows."I all ready benefit from the comfort. So much good has been happening to me lately. God is filling my calendar up with friends-time on the dock and water with friends, time with my sons, getting to know a guy friend, a family from church inviting me to supper, lunch today with a friend, supper tonight at a friend's house to plan a Christian teacher's organization, friends at church asking about me, and a conference at school coming up soon. Next, my calling is to "so that we can comfort those in any trouble with the comfort we ourselves have received from God." God gives me those opportunities so that I may be of comfort to someone else. I want the angels to rejoice in heaven because perhaps I assisted someone to accept Christ. Perhaps I helped them with their every day sufferings with comfort like He has helped me.

June 5 9:30 AM

The title of my diary <u>Believe</u> has changed for me from when I started these journal entries on Feb. 4. Originally it meant I believed my marriage would work. Now Believe means to me "I believe in God, the Father Almighty, creator of heaven and earth." I believe I stand on the solid rock of Christ because all other ground is sinking sand. I believe as Peter did when he stepped out on the water to go to Christ. I believe in miracles and am seeing them daily. I believe in answered prayer. I believe "The Lord says when you search for me you will find me." Jeremiah 29:13 I believe God is showing me the way, the truth, and the life. I believe my Lord is quenching my soul's thirst, feeding me, and making me whole. I believe I love Jesus Christ more than anything in this world. "Did I not tell you that if you believed, you would see the glory of God." John 11:40

June 8 11:00 AM
Lord, right now I am so happy in my life. I love to spend time with you most of all. I love my meditation times, Bible readings, fasting and time with nature. I see you in a child's smile and hear your voice in their laugh. Send me someone who needs me. You are really blessing me, Lord. I am strengthening my ties with my family, friends, Christian friends, and others. I think you are pruning from my life what wasn't clean. I need pruning-bossiness, being judgmental, impatience, too much control in my life. You must be in control, Lord. I long so much for human touch-a hug, holding hands. It has been so long, Lord. My heart is heavy from it. I try not to remember the times in my marriage I was denied those things. I look forward to someone loving me. If this new someone will love God first and foremost, then the rest of our relationship will follow. Teach me to love as I should.

June 9 7:00 AM
The scripture in my quiet time this morning was Hosea 6:1-3. I selected commands for me to do and blessings God would send from the scripture. "Come, let us return to the Lord, He has torn us to pieces but he will heal us; he has injured us but he will bind up our wounds. After two days he will revive us; on the third day he will restore us, that we may live in his presence. Let us acknowledge the Lord; let us press on to acknowledge him, as surely as the sun rises, he will appear; he will come to us like the winter rains, like the spring rains that water the earth."

Let us	He will
Return	heal
Live	bind our wounds
Acknowledge	revive us
Press on	appear
	Come to us

June 10 8:30 AM
I was in a strange mood this morning due to a dream I had about moving, car trouble, my son disobeying me, and general confusion. I don't know why I have to have dreams like that. They seem so real. It must have been all the discussion yesterday with my financial advisor and longtime college friend as I revisited my earliest connections with my ex, told about our separation, and the financial concerns for my future. This morning I am reading Luke 18:14 "For everyone who exalts himself will be humbled, and he who humbles himself will be exalted." A sin of mine is to exalt myself. Lord, you must keep me humble. I feel I am doing better about this but I have a long way to go. I think part of my pride is inherited and the other part is perhaps self-preservation. My ex leaving me and his neglect didn't do a whole lot for my ego. I often felt odd when I would go out in public and notice other men giving me more attention by staring at me than my own husband did. I also noticed how much attention my ex always gave to other attractive women. It is best to forget the past and move on to my future. I found another passage on humility. Philippians 2:3-5 "Do nothing out of selfish ambition or vain conceit, but in humility consider others better than yourselves. Each of you should look not only to your own interests, but also to the interests of others. Your attitude should be the same as that of Christ Jesus."

June 10 9:30 AM

It looks like I just want to journal on everything today. I never would have guessed how much I enjoy doing this where I can get my feelings, frustrations, and joys on paper. It is fun to go back and reread what I have said and to see how I have grown. Forgiveness-Have I truly forgiven my husband? God will not help me if I haven't. Colossians 3:12-14 "Therefore, as God's chosen people, holy and dearly loved, clothe yourselves with compassion, kindness, humility, gentleness, and patience. Bear with each other and forgive whatever grievances you may have against one another. Forgive as the Lord forgave you. And over all these virtues put on love, which binds them all together in perfect unity." This is what I want to live by. Lord, help me to show compassion, kindness, humility, gentleness and patience. Help me to truly forgive any wrong any human has done against me. Don't let anything I do hold me back from your purpose for me in life. Just don't let me because of my human desires mess up.

June 10 11:30 AM

I just stepped out and called my husband at work. I told him I had to get something off my chest and I would have told it to his voicemail but I would tell him. I said, "It doesn't matter what you say to me or do to me I will always remember the love I had for you. I want to thank you for what has happened because otherwise I would not have grown into the person I have become." He said that meant more to him than I realized. He would always regret some of the decisions he had made for the rest of his life. He would always be thankful for the years we had together. I wished him well and we signed off.

June 10 11:50 AM

I don't want to look back on the bitterness of the past any more. God, don't let me relive those hurtful events any more. I am at peace with my present state and I look forward to my future. I am waiting patiently for God to work in my life.

June 14 9:30 AM

Last entry for my journal- make it good. I think my biggest problem is worry. I think it always has been in our marriage and especially in my children's relationships with me in their teen and adulthood years. I think today's scripture hit the nail on the head. Matthew 6:33 "Seek first God's kingdom and his righteousness, and all these things will be given to you as well." If I put God first then he will meet all of my day to day needs. I all ready see evidence of that as he helps me with my finances, tithing, relationships, church work, and my purpose in life. So much has been give to me through nurturing friendships as well. Never have I had such good friends as now. Time and time again friends have supported me and understood me, advised me when I worry, and prayed with me. So many thoughtful deeds have been done for me. My friends look after others first and themselves last.

I saw a full rainbow last week on my way to church. That full rainbow shows a promise for the future and a hope. Jeremiah 29:11 "For I know the plans I have for you, declares the Lord, plans to prosper you and not to harm you, plans to give you hope and a future." I haven't seen many full beautiful rainbows in my life, but I plan to see a lot more. God reveals himself to me in so many ways and I am thankful for that. God also knows what I need. He will provide!

June 17, 2004

God is speaking to me about being patient. The passage that struck me in the Bible study today was Hebrews 11:40 "God had planned something better for us that only together with us would they be made perfect." This passage comes after a listing of all the people in the Bible who had faith enough to believe what God had promised for them. I must have the patience to wait for what God has promised for me. God has something better planned for my life. I just need the patience to wait and let Him lead me there. I am excited about my future because I am experiencing happiness I had lost. I am trying things I haven't done in years. God reveals happiness in the small things: Spending time with friends, talking, praying, and listening are all fun. God has sent me so many friends to talk and listen to. Thank you, Lord, for caring enough about my life to plan my present and future days. I love you!!! "Only together" Only together with you, Lord, will my future be perfect. Keep me focused on heavenly things and not on earthly things. God, you are important in my life.

June 23, 2004

"In returning and rest you shall be saved; in quietness and confidence shall be your strength." Isaiah 30:15 The biggest change in me since this separation is my desire to be alone at times. I used to fear being alone, but now I cherish the times I have to spend alone in meditation with God. I especially enjoy doing that in the beautiful outdoors. Another time is when I wake up in the middle of the night. If I go too long without the meditation time I begin to sense restlessness in me because I haven't spent time with God.

June 23, 2004

Prayer: Lord, if my husband is not the man you want to be with I release him to you. Take him out of my life if we are not to be together. Close the door on this relationship if it is not of you. I am walking step by step with you because I do not want to make another mistake.

As I pray this several times a week I feel God is leading me away from my husband and showing me things about him I do not like. Things are occurring now that make me realize I am better off without my husband. This is a quote I put on my desk calendar. "If I walk step by step with God through each day of my loss in time this pain that seems to be without end will actually subside and I will know happiness." I am amazed at the happiness God is showing me through my friends. I enjoy watersports again and visiting with the club members. I love to ride in the boat and watch others or sit on the dock and visit. I am enjoying skiing more often, trying trick skiing again, and I look forward to other sports. God has blessed me through friendship relationships. I am feeling happiness again.

Journal during separation   June 24, 2004

Psalm 107:4-9 "Some wandered in desert wastelands, finding no way to a city where they could settle." (That is me. I have been wandering my whole life I think. God is now leading me from the wastelands to a city where I can settle. God only knows where that city is for me. I am just trusting Him to show me that city.) v.5 "They were hungry and thirsty and their lives ebbed away. Then they cried out to the Lord in their trouble, and he delivered them from their distress."(I am hungry and thirsty for better things in life: for a better me, for better relationships in a marriage, and with my sons, friends, and church members. God's word is quenching my thirst because He is showing me how to improve myself so that all of these other relationships will work out. I am crying out to my Lord in my times of trouble with divorce and my relationship with my sons. He will deliver me from my distress. I believe that with all my heart, soul, and strength.) v. 7"He led them straight way to a city where they could settle" (the straight way is the path He wishes for me to stay on so that these things will be granted to me. I try not to worry about staying on that path, but I am human and sinful. God has his hands full keeping me straight, but I also believe in my God that He can accomplish whatever He wants in my life. All I have to do is Trust Him and obey Him.)Verse 8 "Let them give thanks to the Lord for His unfailing love and His wonderful deeds for men." (He is doing wonderful deeds for me right now. I cannot remember a time in my life when I have been as happy. God daily shows me the beauty in His word, His creation, and in thoughtful deeds of others as they take care of me. I really don't deserve all of this. God is good! I am gaining discernment in that I asked God to allow me to see the good in others. I see so much of it.) Verse 9 "for He satisfies the thirsty and fills the hungry with good things." (God does satisfy and fills my hunger. I think it is just best to stay hungry and thirsty so that God will continue to show me how to live to quench that thirst and hunger. Thank you, Lord, for satisfying me. You bless me every day!)

June 26, 2004 (6 months into separation)

I am sitting here at a Lake Lure Mountain Retreat with my aunt's family reunion for the weekend. I am looking out over a beautiful golf course and mountain. The sky is overcast. Psalm 36:5-6 "Your love, O Lord, reaches to the heavens your faithfulness to the skies. Your Righteousness is like the mighty mountains, your justice like the great deep." It is hard to even fathom how much love that is. The sky is so endless and expansive above me. I see the strength in the mountain, which is God who grants me righteousness. I can only imagine how deep the oceans are, but I don't have to imagine how great God's love is because He is showing me daily the depth and width, and breadth of his love.

Journal entry during separation   June 27, 2004

I wanted to journal on the scripture at church today. It was amazing that the verse which spoke to me this morning in devotion ended up being the one the minister preached on. Luke 9:62 "Jesus replied, 'No one who puts his hand to the plow and looks back is fit for service in the kingdom of God.'" This spoke to me because I feel like I do look back at the bad parts of my past and they hold me back from my future. I must have God heal me of my past. Give it up-release it to God. Have him take it away. Plow ahead focused on the future and the great plans God has in store for me. It will be far greater than I ever imagined. Trust in God!

Journal entry during separation   July 1, 2004

I had a tough day two days ago when I went to Columbia to find out about my retirement and I changed the beneficiary to my sons rather than my husband. When I left the retirement office I was so depressed at the finality of the whole thing. In this morning's scripture reading Philippians 4:19 was great. "And my God will meet all your needs according to his glorious riches in Christ Jesus." I feel so blessed. Blessed doesn't even begin to describe appropriately what this passage means to me. God has been showing me proof of looking after me in so many ways. He takes care of everything. John 15:7 "If you remain in me and my words remain in you, ask whatever you wish, and it will be given you." The part of this I really want to do is remain in God and his words. Please alleviate any worries I have about my future. Lord, lead me and guide me.

Journal entry during separation   July 2, 2004

Devotion scripture Psalm 30 all of it but specifically verse 5. "For his anger lasts only a moment, but His favor lasts a lifetime; weeping may remain for a night, but rejoicing comes in the morning." How true that is. God always brings us to happiness in the daytime. My weeping has been short but my happinesses have been long. God's favor does last for a lifetime. I am enjoying life so much right now. Thank you, Lord Jesus!

Journal during separation   July 11, 2004

Philippians 3:10 "I want to know Christ and the power of his resurrection and the fellowship of sharing in his sufferings becoming like him in his death, and somehow to attain to the resurrection from the dead." The last part really strikes me as I want to <u>attain</u> to the resurrection. I want to attain resurrection from my old me to my new me. Knowing Christ and suffering like Christ are the two steps here I am told to achieve this. To know Christ is to suffer. Christ suffered so much for us. To suffer for the good of someone else is not suffering. God did this for us by sending his son to die on the cross. Lord, help me to know you. I want to know you in every aspect of my life and get to know you better through my suffering. If I am lonely I think how lonely you were in the Garden of Gethsamene when your closest friends and disciples would not keep watch with you the night before you were crucified. I don't know what suffering is because I haven't been nailed to a cross. I want to <u>know, share, become, and attain.</u> These seem like good steps for getting there.

Journal during separation   July 18, 2004

Hebrews 11:8-12 tells of the faith of Old Testament characters. Noah built an ark because God told him to even though rain had never occurred before. Abraham went to another land because God called him to. Sarah was too old to have a child but by faith she and Abraham had a son. Verse 33 Chapter 11 "By faith these people overthrew kingdoms, ruled with justice, and received what God had promised them." Verse 39-40 "All of these people mentioned received God's approval because of their faith, yet none of them received all that God had promised. For God had far better things in mind for us that would also benefit them, for they can't receive the prize at the end of the race until we finish the race."

I don't know. I seem to be so selfishly focused on my life and what is happening in it right now. I truly want to get beyond that. Divorce, my relationship with my children, selling my house, buying a house, new relationships….Lord, help me to have the faith these OT heroes had and believe in your plan for my future for I know you have far better things in mind for me! I know you didn't mean for me to live a life with a partner who lied to me and made me unhappy constantly. I am already finding the benefits of trusting and obeying you now. If these Bible greats can do it, I certainly can do it. "I can't receive the prize at the end of the race until I finish the race." I'm running, Oh Lord, I'm running forward. Help me be of some good to others so that I may carry them with me on the way.

7 months into separation   July 16, 2004
        Each and every day is incredible in the Lord. Today's scripture is
Psalm 34:1-10. David states what I feel, "I will extol the Lord at all
times; his praise will always be on my lips. I sought the Lord, and he
answered me, he delivered me from all my fears." He is delivering me
from all of my fears about my future. "Those who look to him are
radiant; their faces are never covered with shame." I think if you look at
me you can see God. I am so happy now and I carry myself with such
pride. I feel the presence of the Lord with me. "Taste and see that the
Lord is good; blessed is the man who takes refuge in him." I am taking
refuge in him now. I am blessed by the great things he is allowing to
happen in my life. "For those who seek the Lord lack no good thing." I
feel this is true in my life right now as well. I lack no good thing.

(This entry brought me much comfort with a family situation. God's
timing is perfect all the time!)

Separation   Mission trip journal   July 19, 2004
Mission trip-Our Bible study today was so great because Jesus gave a
woman who was pretty much a social outcast a chance to be somebody
because he offered her good news and living water so that she could share
that with others. John 4:4-15. I feel very closely akin to this woman as I
have been an outcast from my marriage. God has offered me a chance at a
future where I will be able to spread the good news and in turn regain my
self worth. I also feel like her because recently I feel like I have met Christ
personally one on one at the well and He has offered me living water
where I will never thirst again. All I have to do is believe he has my future
in His hands. This mission trip has made me the Samaritan woman. Like
her I had no idea when I came to this mission trip what I might find at the
well. He knows and I'll take away a lot more than just drawing water just
as she got more from her ordinary visit to the well. My life will be
changed. In what ways I do not know, but I just feel that to be true for me.
I must worship God in spirit and in truth like he told her to do. I want to
proclaim God's good news to everyone just like she happily told everyone
in town she had met the Messiah. Jesus was so excited about this convert
he couldn't even eat. He is that excited about me and my future with him
too. I know he loves and cares for me that much.

                                                       July 21, 2004
        Philippians 2:3-11 "Don't be selfish, don't live to make a good
impression on others. Be humble, thinking of others as better than yourself.
Don't think only about your own affairs, but be interested in others too and
what they are doing." I think this is very important to me to think of others,
not to live to impress others, and thinking of others as better than myself.
These are important lessons right now. I should be reminded of verse 5
"your attitude should be the same that Christ Jesus had. Though he was God,
he did not demand and cling to his rights as God, He made himself nothing,
he took the humble position of a slave and appeared in human form. And in
human form he obediently humbled himself even further by dying a
criminal's death on a cross." That is so amazing that Christ humbled himself
in such a manner. I have seen it repeatedly in the scriptures how Christ
humbled himself. I would like to journal on that sometime.

Matthew 17 tells of the father who took his son to the disciples and they couldn't heal him. Jesus rebuked the disciples for their little faith, for if they had faith the size of a mustard seed they could move mountains. Then tax collectors asked Peter if his teacher paid the temple tax. When he asked Jesus about that Jesus sent him to go down to the lake, catch the first fish, open its mouth, and in it will be the coin needed to pay the tax. Jesus had to deal with so much. There were such earthly issues as temple taxes when there were greater things at stake about eternal life and so much more to learn in the short amount of time he had here on earth. It is amazing how he had to prove himself over and over. Lord, please keep me focused on the important things in life and to trust you implicitly with guarding my life. Your miracles and power continue to impress me and impress upon me the desire to be your servant. Lead me in my faith also to be able to move mountains. The problems of this world that seem insurmountable are not when I turn to you in prayer. Connect me to you, Father, so that together we can do great things for this world. I love You! Amen.

Coming home from mission trip   July 25, 2004

I was moved to tears by God's blessings through his word on my return flight. The scripture really touched my heart because it describes exactly how I feel right now. Lamentations 3:19-24 "The thought of my suffering and homelessness is bitter beyond words." This return trip has me feeling homeless. Just what am I calling home now and what am I going home to? No one. Everyone on this trip is so anxious to get home and I am not. I will have to be alone again after I have had such a great opportunity to be around people and having someone to talk to at all times. "I will never forget this awful time, as I grieve over my loss, yet I still dare to hope when I remember this." This loss for me has been my husband, sons, and soon to be home. The reassurance I needed after feeling all of this came from "The unfailing love of the Lord never ends! By his mercies we have been kept from complete destruction. Great is his faithfulness; his mercies begin afresh each day. I say to myself 'The Lord is my inheritance, therefore I will hope in him!' " God's love has never ended for me and I should be ashamed to feel this way about going home. He will provide for me far better than I can imagine. I just hope I won't be let down when I return. I should anticipate renewing my bond with my sons and perhaps starting some new bonds in love relationships. Verse 31 "For the Lord does not abandon anyone forever. Though he brings grief, he also shows compassion according to the greatness of his unfailing love. For he does not enjoy hurting people or causing them sorrow." This should be reassurance enough for me. Praise God for His faithfulness.

5:30 PM   August 23, 2004

2 Timothy 1:12 "That is why I am suffering as I am. Yet, I am not
ashamed, because I know whom I have believed, and am convinced that
he is able to guard what I have entrusted to him for that day." I am not
ashamed to believe in the Lord Jesus Christ as my Master and Savior. I
know whom I believe in. He grants me every breath I take and gives me
my purpose for living. He guards what I entrust to Him each and every
day. And some days it is just so he can get me through that one day. I
entrust each day to Him. He is my shepherd. My name is etched in His
hand.

7:00 AM   August 28, 2004

Last Thursday was the meeting with my husband and his lawyer. My
husband's hands were shaking when he came to the meeting and he sat
and punched numbers on a calculator the whole time our lawyers talked.
We didn't say much at all. We let our lawyers do the talking. I could
really feel God's presence there. I know so many people were praying
about our meeting. It was incredible how the four times I looked over at
my lawyer that he caught my glance as I quietly shook my head no to the
proposals my husband's lawyer was making. I prayed with my lawyer
before our meeting even started. He seemed to appreciate that. God is
guiding me each step of the way. My lawyer wanted me to decide
something by Friday since I disagreed with the settlement. I told him,no,
that I needed to talk to my financial advisor first. Then I told my husband
I wanted to go ahead today and divide up the marital possessions in the
house. His lawyer asked if we would be okay discussing this without
them in the room. I told him we would be fine. My husband asked if I
was really okay and I assured him with a big smile I was. The sense of
peace I had during the whole thing was beyond description.

        Last night I drove to see my boys out of town and even the drive
down was amazing. God provided me with a beautiful full moon to view
out my front windshield the whole way down, great music to listen to,
and a happiness I cannot describe. I was all ready celebrating the future
happinesses that are scriptural about "a promise for a hope and a future."
Sept .8 my divorce will be final, but God is telling me my life is going to
be better. He has all ready given me special events to look forward to.
Who knows what other good things God has in store for me. Labor Day
weekend will be hard because my sons and ex-husband will be at the
beach with extended family. This is an event I have participated in for
the last 24 years. God will provide for me for that weekend as well. If I
stay focused on what I can do for others and not on my own situation
God will see me through.

9:00 PM   Aug. 28, 2004

You won't believe what two prayers I opened to in *The Power of a Praying Parent* by Stormie Omartian. The first was "Destroying an Inheritance of Family Bondage" for my oldest son. It discusses not inheriting the sins of the parent. That relieves me concerning the divorce legacy scripture "Stand fast therefore in the liberty by which Christ has made us free, and do not be entangled again with a yoke of bondage." Galatians 5:1. Also "The Spirit of the Lord God is upon me, because the Lord has anointed me to preach good tidings to the poor; <u>He has sent me to heal the brokenhearted</u>, to proclaim liberty to the captives, and the opening of the prison to those who are bound." Isaiah 61:1 Wow!

My youngest son's prayer was " 'Inviting the Joy of the Lord' praying for the gift of joy, happiness and true joy are only found in Jesus. Deliver him from despair, depression, loneliness, discouragement, anger, or rejection." The scripture was Romans 15:13 "Now may the God of hope fill you with all joy and peace in believing, that you may abound in hope by the power of the Holy Spirit." Also John 15:10-11 "If you keep my commandments, you will abide in my Father's commandments and abide in His love. These things I have spoken to you, that my joy may remain in you, and that your joy may be full." I don't know if these prayers and scriptures were for my sons or me. I benefited from them as well. My joy is that I have God and my two sons.

8:30 AM   Aug. 29, 2004

This morning I read about Jonah. There are some distinct parallels I think in his faith and attitude to mine. I feel Christ is speaking to me through these scriptures. Even while Jonah was in the whale he thought he was drowning, seaweed covered him and weighed him down, yet he believed he would see the temple of God again. I believe I have that kind of faith through this whole divorce thing. The bad part about Jonah is he felt the people of Nineveh should be punished and God had pity on them and rescued them. Jonah went off and pouted in response to this because God didn't do what he wanted him to do. Whoa! Is that me? God leads me and then do I pout because my life isn't working out as <u>I</u> had planned? Divorce wasn't in the picture for me but now I am getting divorced. Selling the house wasn't for me, but I am. Being alone wasn't for me, but I am. The boys believing lies but they are. Questioning how I made the decision originally to marry my husband. I can't do this! Jesus has to heal me of my past and make my way for the future. Philippians 2:5 "Let this mind be in you which was also in Christ Jesus." I didn't see Jesus whining about his destiny to die on the cross. Make my mind like yours, O Lord. Jeremiah 29:11 "For I know the plans I have for you declares the Lord, to honor you and to prosper you to give you a hope and a future." I know these things, Lord. You should <u>not</u> have to remind me of them.

33

10:00 PM   Aug. 30, 2004

Today's scripture was amazing! Deuteronomy 31:1-8 and Isaiah 43:18-19. The Lord said, "Do not remember the former things, or consider the things of old." This is telling me to forget my past, quit talking about it, and move on with my future with God. "I am about to do a new thing; Now it springs forth, do you not perceive it?" God has <u>new</u> plans for me. I must believe in him and listen to him as he tells me what to do. Give me the wisdom and discernment to perceive it. "I will make a way in the wilderness and rivers in the desert." It doesn't matter how impossible it seems God will make a way for me. I have no expectations about my future. I only trust in God to deliver me from this desert. He is so almighty and powerful he can do whatever he wants with my life. He can put rivers in deserts, move mountains, and send hurricanes. I fear the Lord and trust Him.

5:50 PM   Aug. 31, 2004

I was sitting here in my bedroom reading today's devotion and suddenly the sun came over the cloud and shone in on my face. Do I think that is accidental? No, it moved me to tears how God constantly reassures me with his presence. I have had a good day because of <u>Him.</u> Thank you, Lord.

10:00 PM   Sept. 1, 2004

One week today and I will be divorced. DIVORCED, I never, never thought that word would be in my vocabulary. God knows what is best for me though. Two scriptures stood out to me today-Galatians 1:10 "Am I now trying to win the approval of men or of God? Or am I trying to please men? If I were still trying to please men, I would not be a servant of Christ." My mistake was trying to please my husband above God. I now have my priorities straight and I will keep them there if I am allowed to ever have another marriage relationship or any relationship at all. God is number 1 for me and all the others will fall in place. The other scripture is 2 Timothy 2:12 "If we died with him, we will also live with him if we endure, we will also reign with him. If we disown him he will also disown us." I have been dying with him since December. I know I have a long way to go to carry the cross with Christ, but at least I am taking the first steps. I look forward to the living with him parts. He has all ready been showing me his love and grace. If I endure I will reign with him. Reign is a word of victory. I need to reign with him next Wednesday as my husband and I make our financial plans. My king is the Lord Jesus Christ and He reigns in my life. I trust him to handle all of my financial affairs for me. I pray He will be with me in that court room, with my lawyer, and my judge.

11:00 PM   Sept. 2, 2004
2 Corinthians 10:5 "Casting down imaginations and every high thing that
exalteth itself against the knowledge of God, and bring into captivity every
thought to the obedience of Christ." Am I plagued with fearful or angry
thought? No, I am not going to be. My sinful patterns are 1. desires for sex
2. fear of the future, (job, family, money, house)
3. angry thoughts of my husband 4. judgment
Lord, please forgive me of these sins and renew my mind. I want to replace
these thoughts and behaviors with thoughts of you. Forgive me, Lord.

7:30 AM   Sept. 6, 2004
I wanted to journal on the realization I came to. I went out to run. When I
came in I realized with the help of God that I always searched a little
wistfully for something in my marriage that was missing and I couldn't
quite put my finger on it. I am not searching any more. I have found peace
with who I am and where I am right now. I realize I can be alone and be
happy with that. I know I had to come to terms with myself before I could
give my heart to someone else in the future. Thank you, Lord Jesus, for the
sense of peace that only you can give. "Cause me to hear your loving
kindness in the morning, for in you do I trust; cause me to know the way in
which I should walk, for I lift up my soul to you." Psalm 25:1

5:40 AM September 8 – Date of final divorce   Sept. 8, 2004
Daniel 5:27 "You have been weighed in the balances and found
wanting." See my Sept. 6 journal. This passage of scripture speaks to me
today because before I was weighed on the scale and I was wanting more
in my life in my marriage. God has taught me much about peace and
contentment these past few months. I am happier than I have ever been
and the searching has ended. God provides me with all of my wants and
needs. It seems like each day is a new test given by the devil but God
handles my doubt and worry: financially, spiritually, emotionally, and
prayerfully. It is great to know God is fighting my battles for me.

8:00 AM   Sept. 18, 2004
Romans 12:2 "Do not conform any longer to the pattern of this world,
but be transformed by the renewing of your mind. Then you will be able
to test and approve what God's will is –his good, pleasing, and perfect
will." God wants only good for us. I must surrender my mind to Christ to
allow Him to make my decisions for me and love him with all my heart,
mind, soul, and strength. If I turn myself over to him he will decide every
aspect of my life, every step I take. I am standing on that promise now.
Lord, do not allow me to run my life based on my own understandings,
but allow me to be in you and with you so that I may no longer be
myself. I rely on you for every step I take, every word I speak, every
thought I have, every action I do, and every decision I make. Without
you I am nothing. I will trust in you and obey your word. By the power
of the Holy Spirit in me I pray these things. Amen.

7:00 AM   Sept. 19, 2004

In my devotion reading this morning it talked about teaching others to pray. This writer found it difficult until God told her to "pray the scriptures." He had her open to a passage that was just perfect for the girl who was trying to learn to pray. Lord, help me be like that where I will listen to you. Tell me what to do, to act on it, and to make an impact on someone else. The scripture touching my heart today also can make an impact on countless others. 1 Peter 3:15 "Always be prepared to give an answer to everyone who asks you to give the reason for the hope that you have." I want people to see that hope in me to further your work you started in me. "Ask and ye shall receive it." Perhaps, no, I <u>know</u> when I ask for the right things in prayer like this you will grant my request. "Create in me a clean heart, O <u>God</u>, and renew a right spirit within me." Thank you for answered prayers. Amen.

7:00 AM   Sept. 29, 2004

Ten things I was thankful for yesterday

1. Discussion with a guy friend and his honesty in friendship
2. helped friend by allowing her to stay at my house with her bad headache
3. service club meeting at school went well, helping others
4. President of service club is stepping up to do well as leader
5. One of classes at school behaving better
6. Time to pray for my sons
7. My youngest son called. He asked a cooking question
8. Able to catch oldest son on phone as well
9. Had a chance to listen to a friend discuss her problems
10. Enjoyed volleyball match with some of my students on the team
11. Friend called to make plans to go out to eat with her Friday evening

OOPs! Ran over 10. God is blessing me with more than enough. I am blessed with so many opportunities now to listen and help others. Thank you, Lord! My relationship is improving with my boys as well. Help me to be a better servant for you, Christ. Expand my territory, bless me indeed, keep me safe, and keep me away from evil. Amen.

10:30 PM   Sept. 29, 2004

Phil.2:5 "Your attitude should be the same as that of Christ Jesus." It is amazing to me that Jesus allowed himself to suffer the deepest hurt of all- betrayal. He can relate to how I feel and even more. His part of servanthood was to experience this hurt and perhaps I must experience this in order to be more Christlike. I too have suffered in a small manner like Christ. Jesus trusted God through this difficult time and I must too. God, plan to use this mightily for YOU. I am allowing you to take my life and use it. I pray to be Christllike but then I whine about it. Do I choose to fellowship with Christ? Do I trust my God and Father through all of this? YES, YES YES!

7:00 AM   Oct. 4, 2004

I am feeling anxious this morning about everything I must get done about my personal life. I feel rejection from my Dad, my ex- husband, and now I realize someone I am interested in is only to be a friendship. I do so want a relationship with someone who will just be interested enough to show me affection. I miss it so badly. I have that in another friend but he is not the man for me. I don't want to lead him on. I called a friend to pray for me. She showed me Psalm 119:145-152 "I call with all my heart, answer me, O Lord, and I will obey your decrees. I call out to you; save me and I will deep your statutes." I feel that way this morning as I cry out to Him. I plan to obey God's laws for me. "I rise before dawn and cry for help; I have put my hope in your word." This morning I started crying out before dawn and now I am in God's word looking for comfort. "My eyes stay open through the watches of the night, that I may meditate on your promises." This is something I need to do is meditate on His promise. "Hear my voice in accordance with your love, preserve my life, O Lord, according to your laws." This is so reassuring that I am loved. "Those who devise wicked schemes are near, but they are far from your law." The devil is plotting against me this morning to make me feel like there is no hope and only despair. If I am in your law or the word the devil goes away beaten by your promises of hope. "Yet you are near, O Lord, and all your commands are true. Long ago I learned from your statutes that you established them to last forever." My problems are temporary for God is everlasting for He said, "I will never leave you, nor forsake you." Thank you, Lord, for your enduring love for me. It is all I need now and forever.

2:30 PM   Oct. 6, 2004

Wrote this journal entry while at school

2 Chronicles 32:7 "BE strong and courageous! Don't be afraid of the king of Assyria or his mighty army, for there is power far greater on our side! He may have a great army, but they are just men. We have the Lord our God to help us and to fight our battle for us!" This is very encouraging to me today because most of my problems are on the level of "They are just men." Putting my problems into perspective, nothing is that important because I have the Lord, my God to help me and to fight my battles for me. What else do I need other than Him on my side? NOTHING. He is my strength, my shield, my Master, my companion, my all in all. He is the I Am. He created this whole universe and He loves me.

4:30 AM   Oct.7, 2004

I loved my passages of scripture today. "A man's heart plans his way, but the Lord directs his steps." Proverbs 16:9. "Cause me to know the way in which I should walk, for I lift up my Soul to You." Psalm 143:8 "When He the spirit of truth has come, He will guide you into all truth." John 16:13

These verses are so uplifting. I feel like a vessel which needs filling with the Holy Spirit. I want so badly to know more and to have God guide me more and more. I am addicted to His word and I look forward each day to spending time with Him: reading his word, memorizing the word, studying his word, and spending quiet time with him either singing or praying. Thank you for spending time with me, Lord. I love you!

2:15 PM   Oct. 8, 2004

At school

Mark 9:24 "The father instantly replied, 'I do believe, but help me not to doubt.' " Lord, I pray that you will help me not to doubt. Give me the strength to face the loneliness. Give me the sense of peace which only you can give as weekends approach and I have nothing to do on a Friday night. This is also the weekend when my ex is visiting my boys with his girlfriend and her children. I need your strength to deal with this. Thank you for "he orders his angels to protect me wherever I go" and "I will protect those who trust in my name, when they call on me I will answer."

6:30 AM   Oct. 10, 2004

My devotional this morning was talking about being thankful for encouragement from others. As weekends approach and I don't have plans to keep me busy I often get anxious, fretful, and worried about being alone. I attended a dear friend's wedding this past weekend. It was the most beautiful wedding service I had ever attended. I saw several old friends. A pastor from the church where I attended when I first got married was there. He and his wife were both very encouraging about my future. They said they were praying for me. I sat with another dear friend from that church. I ran into some prayer warrior friends of mine and she told me she and her husband were praying for my next mate. I met another blessing when I was introduced to the lady in charge of divorce care at a local church. She was very encouraging to me as well. The Lord was filling my cup. The bride came up to me and made me cry with her comments. She said she and her husband would be attending my wedding and celebrating with me someday. During the ceremony she thought of me when the minister preached on something blue in the wedding and blue represented Christ, the love of Christ, and the royalty of Christ. She thought of how God is working in my life. I was moved that she would think of me during her wedding ceremony. It was great for God to send me all of this support from others. I know he loves me so much.

7:00 AM   Oct. 10, 2004

Romans 15:4 "For everything that was written in the past was written to teach us, so that through endurance and the encouragement of the Scriptures we might have hope." I know that studying God's word will teach me. It was written several thousand years ago and has guided the saints through the years. I want God's word to be imprinted on my heart. Endurance is a key element in my situation right now. Endurance will help me see the race through until God is ready for me to do His will. Endurance is necessary for me to be refined in the fire. In the meantime, until God has me ready the scriptures teach me much and give me the strength to face my trials, Hope is what I attain through all of this. The hope is for my future. Thank you, Lord, for teaching me through the scriptures. I willingly embrace your word and I ask that you give me wisdom, discernment, and revelation concerning the lessons you want me to learn in life. I am thankful for my Master and teacher. I love you.   Amen.

2:45 PM   Oct.11, 2004

What a tremendous idea-God's silence is a sign of intimacy. Can God trust me like that or am I still asking Him for a visible answer? I have been asking for the blessing I want when I should be waiting for an even more wonderful understanding of Christ. He has an even bigger revelation for me. Praise God for the silence. I should be confident that God has heard me. This past weekend I spent much time alone. I spent a good bit of it praying as I mowed grass Saturday and time alone with my dog in the kayak on the water Sunday morning. It was so beautiful that God revealed to me a blue heron, a sliver of the moon in the sky and a star beside it even though the sun had risen. The sky was so vast and beautiful with the clouds spread out like the waves at the beach. The mist was rising from the water. God is so good to reveal his creation to me.

6:30 AM   Oct. 20, 2004

I asked that God teach me through the scriptures this morning and He did. John 1:48-51 when Jesus asked Phillip to call Nathaniel. Nathaniel quizzed Jesus as to how he knew him and he told him what he was just doing before they came up. Nathaniel answered, "Rabbi, you are the Son of God." Jesus said you will see greater things than these. "Truly, Truly I say to you, you will see heaven opened and the angels of God ascending and descending upon the Son of Man. " God is telling me, Marian, if you believe based on what you have all ready seen just wait until I show you what is to come. All I have to do is believe and see the miracles God has in store. He has all ready sent me angels because I found an envelope in my mailbox with twenty dollars in it and no name. Sunday I gave my testimony to my Sunday school class about tithing and I am broke right now with a week yet until payday. Someone drove a long way out here in the country where I live to put that money in my mailbox. My neighbor called last night and told me she sold my old water ski for me. Between that money and the twenty dollars which mysteriously showed up in my mailbox, I have enough money to make ends meet. God PROVIDES! Thank you for the angels you send my way!

7:00 AM   Oct. 21, 2004

Isaiah 26:3 "You shall keep him in perfect peace, whose mind is stayed on you, because he trusts in you."
Psalm 112:7-8 "He will not be afraid of evil tidings; his heart is steadfast, trusting in the Lord. His heart is established; he will not be afraid, until he sees his desire upon his enemies."

God spoke to me this past Sunday concerning my fears. I allowed "evil tidings" of no family to sit with me at church, a family function-church picnic and me with no one to go with, and boys not coming by to visit on their way home. All of these thoughts were put there to haunt me. God fixed all of that. If I had just had the faith to trust in Him then even if it didn't work out like I planned I would still be in God's hands. I went to the Church picnic with my church family, I am never alone at church because I have my church family, and the boys did come by to see me on the way home. If I had put my faith in God I would have known he would solve all of my problems. My heart will be steadfast in the future, Lord!

I had been praying for God to send me someone who needed me to help them through hard times like I've had. A friend of mine introduced me to a friend of theirs who needed some encouragement. She had suffered divorce years ago and now she feels she is losing her son by letting him meet his father and spend time with him, and her business is doing poorly financially. She helped train a girl and then the girl stole all her clients. She was at a real low point. I talked with her for over an hour and then my friend, my new friend, and I prayed. My new friend and I made plans to go out dancing for last night. I wasn't sure how God was going to use this but I prayed about it very much before we left. I met her and another friend of hers. On our ride all three of us talked about our divorces and the similarities. It was a healing time for us. I can't believe what unexpected thing happened there. I had the time of my life!!! We all spotted this one guy alone. I wanted to dance with him but didn't have the nerve to ask him. My new friend took me over to him and said my friend wants to dance with you. Well he did and we danced at least a dozen times before the night was over. He was the perfect gentleman and the perfect size. Never once did I step on his feet. He taught me how to twostep. Man, can he dance! He told me he was in the Marine Reserves and he had just gotten back from Iraq on a three week leave. We took him to his hotel afterwards because I was worried about his driving. I drove his truck and the girls followed us. He was so handsome. He wanted me to spend the night. He said he would bring me home tomorrow. I told him no, but left him my cell phone number and told him to call me sometime.. We had more time to talk and visit as we drove there. I was so happy. I got in the car with my girlfriends. It was so tempting to stay. The funny thing is the scriptures I read today was Romans 8:3-6 "For God has done what the law, weakened by flesh, could not do: sending his own son in the likeness of sinful flesh and for sin he condemned sin in the flesh, in order that the just requirement of the law might be fulfilled in us, who walk not according to the flesh but according to the Spirit. For those who live according to the flesh set their minds on the things of the flesh, but those who live according to the Spirit set   their minds on the things of the Spirit. To set the mind on the flesh is death, but to set the mind on the Spirit is life and peace."

Wow! I opt for the life and peace myself. I feel like I passed a test last night. Thank you God, for blessing me with the good time, for allowing me to meet this great guy to have fun with last night, and to give me the out so that I would do what was right. I don't know why I was to meet him but he has a lot on him with his leadership role in the military. He told me he had to send young men home in body bags. I will pray for him!

4:00 PM   Oct. 31, 2004

Hebrews 6:18-19 "It is impossible for God to lie, we who have fled to
take hold of the hope offered to us may be greatly encouraged. We have
this hope as an anchor for the soul, firm and secure." God has never lied
to me about a promise of hope for the future and not to harm me in any
way. Sometimes I have "fled to take hold of this hope offered to me."
Today I am boldly taking hold of the hope and the future he has in store
for me. "This hope is an anchor for my soul, firm and secure." Secure
means that it will be there for me. All I have to do is believe in God and
his promises and not doubt when the devil puts doubt in my head. I love
the Lord with al my heart, mind, soul, and strength. Thank you, Jesus.

11:30 PM   Nov. 1, 2004

I wanted to journal on a passage of scripture from my devotions. 1
Thessalonians 5:15-18 "See that none of you repays evil for evil, but
always seek to do good to one another and to all. Rejoice always, pray
constantly, give thanks in all circumstances; for this is the will of God in
Christ Jesus for you." I was pleased to see that in Daddy's Bible he had
underlined this with pencil and put a check mark by it too. This really
made me feel like Daddy was with me today. It is very special to get to
use his Bible. I am happy to find out this was one of his favorite
scriptures.

10:30 AM Election Day   Nov. 2, 2004

Jeremiah 8:5-6 "Why then has this people turned away in perpetual
backsliding? They hold fast to deceit, they refuse to return. I have given
heed and listened, but they have not spoken aright; no man repents of his
wickedness saying, 'What have I done?' Everyone turns to his own
course, like a horse plunging headlong into battle." Lord, this is me
plunging headlong into battle and I have not listened. This is me and MY
country. We have been holding fast to deceit and the USA has been
backsliding. Today I pray for this deceit to end in my country and for my
country to return to You, O Lord and Savior. I want to heed and listen
and so does my country. Make us repentant enough to ask, "What have I
done?" Show us our wrongs and set us on the path of righteousness,.
These things I ask in your Holy name. Amen.

6:00 AM   Nov. 4, 2004

Yesterday bills seemed to pile up as I received a huge tax notice on the house I am still living in because we have not been able to sell it yet. I must split this with my ex-husband. I just called and left him a message on his cell phone to please pay the tax bill because I didn't know where I was going to get the money. Today's scripture is 1 John 1:5-7 "…That God is light and in Him is no darkness at all. If we say we have fellowship with him while we walk in darkness, we lie and do not live according to the truth, but if we walk in the light, as he is in the light we have fellowship with one another." I choose to walk in the light with the Lord. He will lead me in wisdom and discernment in his light to know how to handle these financial burdens. "God is light and in Him is no darkness at all."

11:00 PM   Nov.5, 2004

Last night a prayer warrior friend of mine called and prayed with me. One of the things she said I needed to do was pray for my ex-husband and bless him. I don't have any problem with that because I often pray for him and his girlfriend. In today's devotion the scripture was Luke 6:27-28 "Love your enemies, do good to those who hate you, bless those who curse you, pray for those who mistreat you." That wasn't ironic; that was God-ordained to have that scripture this morning. I am trying to do what is right. Lord, help me.

9:30 AM   Nov. 6, 2004

Today I read in Psalms 119:18 "Open my eyes that I may see wonderful things in your law." Verse 20 "My soul is consumed with longing for your laws at all times." Verse 28 "My soul is weary with sorrow, strengthen me according to your word." Verse 29 "Keep me from deceitful ways; be gracious to me through your law." Verse 30 "I have chosen the way of truth; I have set my heart on your laws." Verse 32 "I run in the path of your commands for you have set my heart free." The setting my heart free really hit me and strengthening me according to his word. God ,I know you are setting my heart free from earthly relationships and I am seeking divine ones.

9:00 AM   Nov.7, 2004

Hebrews 12:28-29 "Therefore, since we are receiving a kingdom that cannot be shaken, let us be thankful, and so worship God acceptably with reverence and awe, for our God is a consuming fire." The cross reference is Deut. 4:23-24 "Be careful not to forget the covenant of the Lord your God that he made with you; do not make for yourselves an idol in the form of anything the Lord your God has forbidden. For the Lord your God is a consuming fire, a jealous God." Perhaps I made an idol of my relationship with my ex- husband. I tried so hard to save the marriage and I invested all of my energies in that area. It seemed the closer I tried to draw to him the farther away from me he pulled. God is a jealous God. He has my undivided attention now. He has been straining me in the fire to get the impurities out.

11:00 PM   Nov.9, 2004
"Gather my saints together to Me, those who have made a covenant with
me by sacrifice." Psalm 50:5
Lord, I make a covenant with you tonight to stand by your side. I will not
break this covenant. I sacrifice who I am to be who you want me to be. I
give up my past life to look forward to the future. I trust my future with
you. Lord, I love you so much. Thank you for answering my prayers.

7:30 AM   Nov. 13, 2004
The Scripture in the devotion was Mark 8:23-25 Jesus laid his hands on a
blind man's eyes and he asked if he could see. The blind man could
partially see. Then Jesus put his hands on the blind man's eyes one more
time and then the blind man could fully see. I feel I am that blind man.
God has me where I can partially see and eventually He will allow me to
fully see. That may not be until I am in heaven with Him but he will
reveal to me all the truths about why I had to divorce. Prayer "Holy God,
continually redirect my vision toward things eternal." Amen. Another
devotion book I use had this scripture. Wow! It goes right along with the
other "The commandment of the Lord is pure, enlightening the eyes."
Psalm 19:7-8

10:00 PM   Nov.15, 2004
Genesis 3:8-9 "Then the man and his wife heard the sound of the Lord
God as he was walking in the cool of the day, and they hid from the
Lord God among the trees of the garden." Lord, please don't let me hide
from you. I want to walk in the direction you are going with YOU. "But
the Lord God called to the man,'Where areYou?' " Lord, I am here. I am
listening to your voice. Thank you for your love and concern as to where
I am. Thank you for wanting me to walk with you. I am so humbled and
honored that you love me that much.

6:00 AM   Nov.17, 2004
IST ANNIVERSARY WITHOUT MY HUSBAND /WOULD HAVE
BEEN 25TH
Psalm 40:5 "Many, O Lord my God are the wonders you have done. The
things you planned for us no one can recount to you; were I to speak and
tell of them, they would be too many to declare." This is so reassuring
today on what would have been my 25th wedding anniversary. God has
done so many wonders in my life. The things He has planned for me are
too good to ever tell. There are too many good plans He has for my life.
One of them is I asked my students to journal yesterday. I read one class
and wrote their prayer requests in a prayer log. It is incredible the
problems they each have. I know God is leading me to pray for each and
every one of my students. That will be so powerful for the glory of God.
Thank you, Lord, for leading me through troubled waters and my
students too.

10:00 PM   Nov. 17, 2004

I had to journal about the sense of peace I felt all day. I know I must have received eight phone calls from friends praying for me. I never once cried because God has me optimistic about my future. I met my ex's mother and stepfather in a town between where they live and I live to eat supper. It was great getting to visit with them. God has led me to encourage others through my own hard times. I shared the Psalms passage with them from Psalms 73; 23-28. They liked it too. "Yet I am always with you; you hold me by my right hand. You guide me with your counsel, and afterward you will take me into glory. Whom have I in heaven but you? And earth has nothing I desire besides you, my flesh and my heart may fail, but God is the strength of my heart and my portion forever. Those who are far from you will perish; you destroy all who are unfaithful to you. But as for me, it is good to be near God. I have made the Sovereign Lord my refuge. I will tell of all your deeds." Wow! Thank you for that word to encourage me, Lord.

9:00 PM   Nov. 20, 2004

Here it is a Saturday night and I am content to be at home reading the Bible. Hebrew 8:6, 12 "He is also Mediator of a better covenant, which was established on better promises. I will be merciful to their unrighteousness, and their sins and their lawless deeds I will remember no more." Lord, I know this means living in the New Testament instead of the Old. Because of Christ sacrifices are no longer needed and God's laws are written in our minds and hearts but not in a code. I interpret this to relate to my life. You are going to give me a covenant with another marriage partner where the promises will mean something. And my past I give up for the new. I anticipate your not remembering my lawless deeds. Thank you, Lord for the future blessings I will receive in a new covenant.

8:30 AM Thanksgiving weekend   Nov.23, 2004

In Luke 5:12-16 Jesus heals a man with leprosy, tells him not to tell anyone, but for him to show the priests, and serve as a testimony to them. Are the priests and I alike in that it takes a healing to believe in God? Do miracles have to be performed in order for me to believe? Verse 15 "Yet the news about him spread all the more so that crowds came to hear him and to be healed of their sicknesses." Could the sicknesses not just be physical sicknesses but also sicknesses of the soul? Verse 16 is interesting "But Jesus often withdrew to lonely places and prayed." Could all the selfish demands of people become overwhelming? I think the lesson here for me is to withdraw to lonely places and pray. If I don't get that quiet time with God I miss it. It is necessary, vital, important for me to have it now. I need you, Lord.

Thanksgiving Day has passed. Only one holiday left for a first since my husband left and I am sure they will get easier as time goes on. The hardest part about it is not having our family together. I heard a country song tonight with the lyrics about a man who lives in an apartment and hates his life because he isn't with his wife, kids, and at home any more. I can't help but wonder if my ex ever feels that way. My boys came home last night. The oldest stayed a few minutes and left. I only saw him for a few minutes today. The youngest slept until about 11:30 and when he was awake he played a video game and didn't talk. Early afternoon their Dad came and took them to his family to celebrate for Thanksgiving. I went down to the dock for some prayer time with God. I didn't cry or anything. I think God is healing me. I called my neighbor friends and they said to come on over to eat Thanksgiving with them. My mother and I went. It was so nice to be with their family! Mother and I had a good time. About 9:30PM the boys stopped back by. They left their dad out in the truck. I was assured they would spend some time with me tomorrow. I called a friend to pray with me about how little time the boys are here. Mama and I had some Bible study time together to get our minds and souls in the right place before going to bed. We needed that. I shared with her how much she means to me!

The way I perceive my divorce was God saving me from a sinking ship. What I thought was so terrible to end this marriage has turned out to be blessings so numerous I cannot count them. This past few days with my mother and my sons has been wonderful. I had the support of family members I love so much. It was so much fun to cook again, laugh, and kid each other. My boys were in the best moods. Mother and I spent each evening doing this Bible study, reading scripture, and praying together. It was wonderful! The pie baking project for the homeless and needy with my service club at high school was a huge success! We baked over 100 pies to donate to a local restaurant that sponsors free Thanksgiving meals each year. My boys, my mom and I went to visit an elderly shut-in friend of mine. That really made her day. She has macular degeneration, much hearing loss, and her legs are so swollen she can hardly walk, but her mind is as clear as a bell. She all ready felt like she knew my family because I had talked about them so much. Mom and I attended a local church and heard a great message on Isaiah about the wolf lying with the sheep and the babies near the cobra with no animosity. Peace is in my heart like it was pictured in that scripture and thankfulness for this wonderful Thanksgiving season. The way I approach life is so different now. The enemy has not been able to defeat me. Lord, be the watchman of my mind. Isaiah 65:17 "Behold, I will create new heavens and a new earth. The former things will not be remembered, nor will they come to mind." This is what you have done with me, Lord. Thank you. Praise his name.

7:00 PM   Dec. 1, 2004

Revelation 21:2-5 "I saw the Holy City, the new Jerusalem, coming down out of heaven from God, prepared as a bride beautifully dressed for her husband." I have been told by my counselor that as Christians we are to be brides for Jesus Christ. I feel like I am His bride saving myself for Him. I want to thank Him for taking me as His bride. With His love I am fine. I will always have His love unlike human love that will pass. Verse 3 "And I heard a loud voice from the throne saying, 'Now the dwelling of God is with men, and he will live with them.' " I am excited that God now lives with me. I am not alone here. He will make my decisions for me. "They will be His people, and God himself will be with them and be their God." That is just what I said. God is with me and I am one of His people. Verse 4 "He will wipe every tear from their eyes. There will be no more death or mourning or crying or pain, for the old order of things has passed away." My old order of things was my marriage to my ex husband. His selfishness overwhelms me. He could care less about my happiness. Today the house showed and the realtor is confident we will get an offer. I called my ex out of politeness to tell him. He was happy. I said, "Well, at least one of us is happy." This will be another test of my trust in God. He knows what is <u>best</u> for His bride. "There will be no more death or mourning or crying or pain for the old order of things has passed away." This house is a stronghold of mine and I give it up to the Lord. There will be other places to live. I have moved many times in my life and I can move again. I look forward to no more death, mourning, crying, or pain. LORD, I TRUST IN YOU!!!

6:00 AM   Dec. 2, 2004

Hebrews 11:6 "And without faith it is impossible to please God, because anyone who comes in him must believe that He exists, and that He rewards those who earnestly seek him." How do I earnestly seek you, Father? I know that I do. I look forward with anticipation being with you every day. Teach me the way, the truth, and the light. I need you to instruct me, fill me, be me so that I do what is pleasing in your sight. My utmost desire is to please you. Forgive me when I am not humble but more importantly forgive me when I fear. You are with me every step of my way and you know what is best for me. If the house sells, it sells. You have allowed me to live here way past the summer, which was what I asked for. Thank you for showering your blessings on me, Lord, I can't afford to stay here and you know that. I love You!

Psalm 37:23-24 "Our steps are made firm by the Lord, when he delights in our way, though we stumble, we shall not fall headlong, for the Lord holds us by the hand." Am I making spiritual steps with God? Does God delight in my spiritual progress?

Isaiah 55:6 "Seek the Lord while he may be found; call on him while he is near." Verse 9 "As the heavens are higher than the earth, so are my ways higher than your ways and my thought than your thoughts." Verse 11 "So is my word that goes out from my mouth. It will not return to me empty, but will accomplish what I desire and achieve the purpose for which I sent it." Lord, thank you for sending me passages of scripture to inspire me. Thank you for caring enough about me "to delight in my way even though I stumble." Thank you for holding me by the hand. I am calling on you while you are near. Keep my thoughts on you because staying focused on you is the right way. Make your word return to you through me as a vessel that is full. Accomplish what you desire in me. Don't let me run ahead of your plan for me by being distracted by temptations. Achieve the purpose for which you sent me. Teach me through your loving guidance and discipline me when I am wrong. Thank you for these things. I ask it all by the power of the Holy Spirit in me. Amen.

7:00 AM   Dec. 20, 2004

Philippians 2:3 "Do nothing out of selfish ambition or vain conceit, but in humility consider others better than yourselves… look to the interests of others… God made himself nothing taking the very nature of a servant." Verse 9 "Therefore God exalted him to the highest place and gave him the name that is above every name, that at the name of Jesus every knee should bow… and every tongue confess, that Jesus Christ is Lord." Hymn 177 Methodist Hymnal "He is Lord, He is Lord, He is risen from the dead and He is Lord. Every knee shall bow every tongue confess that Jesus Christ is Lord." Today I want to take on a new heart of servanthood and humility. I want to be more Christlike. God lead me to do the things you want me to do. I want to be a servant of God following your lead with no selfish ambition or vain conceit. Keep me focused on heavenly things and not earthly things. Don't let me think on a future mate and my aloneness, but on your face and seeking your kingdom. Romans 8:6 "For to be carnally minded is death, but to be spiritually minded is life and peace." Thank you for your guiding word, Lord. I am complete in you. Amen.

6:00 PM   Dec. 23, 2004

I am waiting for my sons to get home. I have been reading about Joseph and how he resisted Potiphar's wife. She tried to seduce him. Temporary gratification is destructive. Intimacy without covenant is merely a lie. It just becomes gratification for the moment. Consequences come from seeking temporary gratification. One of my weaknesses is my joy at being touched, held, cuddled, and loved. I miss that so much. I need to just be honest about my weaknesses with Christ. He will see me through the lonely times and offer me ways out of situations with men I should not be in. Dear Lord, help me through the tough, lonely times when I desire. I love loving someone and I anticipate a Godly man in my future who will help me through such times and honor me as much as I honor him. I want a man who seeks God first and me second. I want a man who does not lie and is deceitful to me. I have been lied to enough in life and I seek the truth. Thank you for the truth in you. Amen.

6:30 PM   Dec. 23, 2004

Genesis 39:23 "I read the story of Joseph in the Bible. He was sold to slavery, put in charge of Potiphar's household, resisted daily temptations to sleep with Potiphar's wife, accused wrongly, thrown in jail, blessed even in jail because the Lord found favor in him. Talk about trials and still making the best of things! God is really using him and growing him through these difficult times. Genesis 39:23 … "because the Lord was with Joseph and gave him success in whatever he did." I feel that God is with me like that because he is giving me favor in whatever I do. I still face trials and troubles but God is there with me through all of this. I love you, Lord Jesus!

8:30 AM   Dec. 25, 2004

I want to journal on 2 passages of scripture this morning. 1.   2
Corinthians 9:15 "Thanks be to God for his indescribable gift!" It cannot
even be put into words the gift that God gave us through His son Jesus
Christ. What more perfect gift could we receive than that on this
Christmas Day. Also 2. 1 Peter 2:4-6 "As you come to Him, the living
stone-rejected by men (I was rejected by my husband and at times my
sons) but chosen by God and precious to him-(this is reassuring that the
one I need most does not reject me, God loves me now and forever) You
also, like living stones, (He is comparing me to Him who is the living
stone)are being built into a spiritual house (I pray, Lord, you will build
me into a spiritual house) to be a holy priesthood, offering spiritual
sacrifices acceptable to God through Jesus Christ (Lord, make me a
living sacrifice to you. Take my life and use me as the sacrifice) For in
scripture it says,'See, I lay a stone in Zion, a chosen and precious
cornerstone, and the one who trusts in him will never be put to shame.' "
(I believe this, Lord. Thank you for calling me precious. Make me like
the cornerstone.)

11:30 AM   Jan. 1, 2005

Luke 1:37 "For nothing is impossible with God." What a great way to
start a new year. God can take even me, a lowly sinner and make
something good come of it. He can take my life and use it in some way
to glorify God. For with Him nothing is impossible! Romans 8:28 "And
we know that in all things god works for the good of those who love him
who have been called according to his purpose." Lord, call me to your
purpose. 2 Chronicles 20:12 "I do not know what to do, but my eyes are
upon you."

1:30 PM   Jan. 1, 2005

Philippians 2:5-11 "Who being in very nature God, did not consider
equality with God something to be grasped, but made himself nothing,
taking the very nature of a servant, being made in human likeness. And
being found in appearance as a man, he humbled himself and became
obedient to death- even death on a cross." I see commands in this God
revealed to me

1. 1st make myself nothing
2. take the very nature of a servant
3. humble myself
4. become obedient

I hear you, Lord! Thank you for revealing things to me in your Word.

2:00 PM   Jan. 2, 2005

John 10:10 "I have come that they may have life, and have it to the full."
"I have come that they may have life and have it more abundantly." God
wants me to experience joy and to experience joy more abundantly. He
wants happiness for me in my life.

6:00 AM   Jan.13, 2005
Isaiah 40:31 "Those who wait for the Lord shall renew their strength, they shall mount up with wings like eagles, they shall run and not be weary, they shall walk and not faint." Right now I must wait for the Lord. I feel like I am running ahead of the Lord. I must renew my strength with God. He will carry me up with eagles high and soaring above anything a human can think of. I would be able to run and not get tired if I wait on God. I will never feel faint or weak because he will give me strength. I pray these things in Jesus' name and for His Holy Sake. Amen.

7:00 AM   April 2, 2005
Luke 13:34 "O Jerusalem, O Jerusalem, you who kill the prophets and stone those sent to you, how often have I longed to gather your children together, as a hen gathers her chicks under her wings, but you were not willing!" Lord, don't ever let me be not willing. I want to draw close to you and learn more and more about your protective love. Thank you for the beautiful sunlight shining in on my Bible and me as I do this devotion.

9:30 AM   April 4, 2005
Saturday God truly blessed me. After the closing on the house from Friday, God put it on my heart to pay for a friend's plane ticket for a mission trip to China. This will be my tithing from the sell of the house. I called to tell my friend and she cried. She said we had to pray about it. I told her I knew that ideas just didn't come into my head. God put it there. God gave me my confirmation today when I was flipping through the pages of a devotional book. I came across a special insert with this scripture printed on a beautiful color page. Proverbs 31:16 "She considers a field and buys it; out of her earnings she plants a vineyard." I broke down in humble tears immediately and called to tell my friend. This is the vineyard-my friend going to China! Praise the Lord for the earnings which allowed me to do that.

3:30 AM   April 22, 2005
Matthew 11:36 "A man's enemies will be the members of his own household." This sounds like me. "Anyone who loves his father or mother more than me is not worthy of me, any one who loves his son or daughters more than me is not worthy of me. And anyone who does not take his cross and follow me is not worthy of me. Whoever finds his life will lose it, and whoever loses his life for my sake will find it." I have taken up my cross to lose my husband, house and sons at times. God promises if I lose my life for His sake He will help me find a better life. I am celebrating that assurance right now.

5:00 PM   April 24, 2005

Acts 16:31 Paul and Silas answered, "Believe on the Lord Jesus, and you will be saved, you and your household." I believe God is going to fulfill this promise to me. I do believe on the Lord Jesus, I have been saved, and my household will be too. Today after church I went out to eat with Tony and Carol. It is so interesting to discuss divorces with other people. The stories are all the same because Satan doesn't have to use anything different. We had a great time talking and I told them I had read in my journal from a year ago that they had stopped by on a difficult afternoon here at the house and how much I had needed them. I told them I still need them one year later. God blessed me with a great day with my boys yesterday and then today when Sunday afternoons are hard, God sent me Tony and Carol. I thank the Lord for his many blessings.

9:30 AM   May 9, 2005

Hebrews 13:5 "Be content with what you have, because God has said 'Never will I leave you; never will I forsake you.' " I must enjoy all seasons of my life. The one I am in right now is to be alone, be happy with it, and find God. He will teach me how to do without the sense of touch from a man and the satisfaction of sex, to be desired, to be desirable. These are things I miss in my aloneness and not having someone to confide in. God is there for me now and he knows my every need. God teach me to savor the season of life I am in. Teach me to reach out to you for comfort and to lift my arms in praise. Amen.

4:00 PM   May 9, 2005

1 John 1:7 "But if we walk in the light, as he is in the light, we have fellowship with one another, and the blood of Jesus his Son, purifies us from all sin." Don't hide what I am. Anything with "I" in it is sin. Don't hide yourself from anyone you should be in fellowship with. And here I was beating myself up over my revealing who I was to my spouse. I thought I should have kept more to myself. I am an open book. I cannot hide my feelings well. Jesus wants me to join with someone to open my heart to with confession and praise for God together. He will show me who this person will be because I never had that in my marriage. My ex-husband always kept himself hidden in the dark and did not let me get to know him. I look forward to a mate I can share with.

(I went from May 9 until June 15 before I even wrote another journal entry.)

12:30 PM   June 15, 2005

Obviously it has been a long time since I have written in this journal. A friend told me he had been reading in Ecclesiastes lately so I read there today. Ecc. 5:1-2 "As you go into the temple, keep your ears open and your mouth shut. Don't be a fool who doesn't even know it is sinful to make rash promises to God. For he is in heaven and you are only here on earth, so let your words be few." "Being a fool makes you talk too much." This hit me. I don't want to make any rash promises to God. I have noticed I talk less since the divorce. This is good because I need to be quiet and listen to friends to hear what their needs are rather than their having to listen to mine. Also, Ecc. 5:20 "To enjoy your work and to accept what you have in life is a gift from God. The person who does that will not need to look sadly on his past. For God gives him reasons for joy." I have learned to look happily on my past with the good memories with my husband and the great memories of being a mother. God gives me reasons for joy each and every day.

8:30 AM   June 20, 2005

Exodus 14:13 "Moses answered the people, 'Do not be afraid. Stand firm and you will see the deliverance the Lord will bring you today. The Egyptians you see today you will never see again." I should wait for the deliverance the Lord will bring me to. I am to stand firm on my rock of salvation and let him attain my victories.   Isaiah 30:15 "This is what the Sovereign Lord, the Holy One of Israel, says: 'In repentance and rest is your salvation, in quietness and trust is your strength, but you would have none of it." Verse 18 "Yet the Lord longs to be gracious to you; he rises to show you compassion. For the Lord is a God of justice. Blessed are all who wait for him." Again here is the waiting part. I am waiting for God to do his will in my life. God will give me the strength to face my difficulties.(I underlined these parts in my journal for emphasis on important words.)

3:15 PM   June 21, 2005

Moment by moment obedience is the goal. God can walk on the storms of my life right now. Stay calm in the middle of turmoil. Mark 6:51 "Then he climbed into the boat with them, and the wind died down. They were completely amazed." It wasn't until the disciples cried out that he came to them. Verse 48 says "He was about to pass them by." Lord, let me cry out to you and not let you pass me by. Thank you for being with me through the storms of life. As I read this scripture a violent thunderstorm was outside, yet I felt safe with you. Only God can walk on the storms. I am not alone facing these scary things. I am with you.

Devotions

A Love like That

A blessing by the name of Robert Sibernaller came into my life over a year ago. A Christian friend asked for prayer for a friend of hers who had broken his right arm, his wife died, and then he fell and broke his left shoulder and leg. He had no children and no relatives in the area to visit him at the hospital so he was all alone. The voice in my head said, "Marian, you need to get involved in that." I told my friend to arrange for me to meet him. A mutual friend of mine and Bob's took me initially to meet him at the hospital. I asked if I might be his friend. He granted me that. I visited him twice a week every week at the nursing home. He was a bit confused about his surroundings at first. One warm, fall evening I made arrangements to wheel him outside in a recliner type wheel chair to eat his supper. (He couldn't sit up or he would topple over with the broken bones he had.) I had to feed him because he couldn't get his arms up to his face. I could tell he was more sad than usual that day. He stopped me from feeding him and asked where his wife was. I stopped, asked God silently for the words to say and explained to him, "Bob, Dot is in a much better place with Jesus where there are no tears and no suffering." Reality set in and tears streamed down his face. Because he could not do so, I wiped his tears for him. It was all I could do to keep from balling myself, but God wasn't through with what he would have me say to him. I lifted his hand, showed him his wedding band and said, "You see this band. It is a symbol of the unending love she has for you and the love you will always have for her." Later when I left the nursing home I wept. God had given me the strength at the time I needed it for him. That in itself was a miracle because I am a very emotional person. I asked God what that was all about. I believe His reply to me was He wanted to show me an example of what one man's love could be for his wife and that one day I would have someone to love me like that too. Thank you, Lord, for showing me a love like that, but more importantly the peace you give me, because YOU love me like that. 1 Corinthians 13:13 "And now these three remain: faith, hope and love. But the greatest of these is love."

Time alone with Jesus

Mark 4:34 "He did not say anything to them without using a parable. But when he was alone with his own disciples, he explained everything." Spending that alone time with Jesus is so important. In all the hustle and business of the world with work, meetings, sports, and social engagements how do we expect to learn from Jesus if we do not spend time alone with him? Allow Jesus to claim you as one of his disciples, spend time alone with him, and allow him to explain everything. Job had to suffer some difficult times of losing everything before he learned some valuable lessons. In Job 23:12 he said, "I have treasured the words of His mouth more than my necessary food." Do you think we could stand to learn something from this? When I have begun to eat a meal I have thought many times do I place a priority on being in the Word listening to what Jesus has to teach me more than the desire to eat? I question my priorities in life. How difficult can it be to set aside time every day to just be in His word and allow Jesus to sit with me and teach me? I believe in doing that he will be more inclined to spend the rest of the day with me because I desire to be with Him.

Forgive me as I remind you of the familiar saying all _ _ _ _ _ breaking loose. Let's turn that around for the good by saying, "All heaven's breaking loose." I believe it is a time of signs, miracles, and wonders. While my mom was at the hospital God reminded me that in my darkest hour of need for me to take the fous off of myself. I did it before during my divorce and it really helped so why wouldn't it now? Several days of spending moments of getaway from the hospital room in the lobby allowed me to witness a young woman in her early 30's surrounded by friends and church members coming to her aid. Once she was alone. I introduced myself and asked her if she minded sharing her story. Her young husband had a rare disease which attacked his neurological system and left this once very athletic man paralyzed from the waist down. The doctors didn't know if he would ever recover. I asked if I could pray with her. She cried openly and thanked me for the prayer. The next day I was able to go to her husband's room and pray with him. He was just as appreciative. The day after that Mom was whisked away to Intensive Care because of a respiratory attack. The decision was to put her on a ventilator That along with heart and digestive problems left her unconscious for several days. After two days in ICU I thought often of the young couple and decided to go see if they were still at the hospital. The young wife made me wait at the door. When she opened the door her husband had just walked to the restroom and was sitting up in a chair. I hugged him with tears of joy! WHAT A MIRACLE! He gave all the credit to God and to the prayers that had been lifted up to God on his behalf. I gave him my Mom's worn devotional book. He knew her condition and treasured it. He didn't just hold it, he clutched it to his chest because he realized how dear it was.

I left that room praising God for miracles. It was just the encouragement I needed during that troubling time. Matthew 18:18 "I tell you the truth, whatever you bind on earth will be bound in heaven, and whatever you loose on earth will be loosed in heaven." I'll tell you to look for heaven breaking loose because God is a God of miracles. If you let loose and believe on earth that miracles can happen it will be loosed in heaven. Believe it! All heaven's breaking loose!

Are You an Answered Prayer?

I have been humbled to hear friends tell me recently they were praying for a friend and I came along. The amazing thing is I feel like their friendship was more of a blessing to me than I was for them. The cross is a perfect example of friendship. The vertical portion is primary in importance because it points up to heaven. A friend will show you by example how important it is in life to look to God first for answers, direction, and instruction. The friend says, "Look up first and I'll be there with you on your journey." This is the horizontal portion of the cross. The horizontal friend is the one who supports you, is a mentor to you, and exhorts you when necessary. Have you noticed how that friend is ironically in the same places of life you are? It happens over and over again. That is so you can parallel each other. As the crossbar of the cross is parallel to the ground that friend truly understands what you are going through because they are there too as an accountability partner sent from God. Ephesians 5:2 "I walk in love, (esteeming and delighting in others) as Christ loved me and gave Himself up for me, a slain offering and sacrifice to God (for me, so that it became) a sweet fragrance." Thank you, Lord, for the friends who walk in love like Christ giving of themselves as a sweet sacrifice for me. Allow me to be an answered prayer by being a friend like that to someone else.

In response to "Are You an Answered Prayer"

I called the local chaplain of Mobile Meals and read aloud my devotion to him on friendship in "Are You an Answered Prayer." He told me how timely that was (a God thing) as he had befriended a guy who had been in prison for two years, was out, got in trouble again, and would soon be going back to prison. Recently the chaplain's family had welcomed him into their home and fed him supper. Afterwards he lost control and the chaplain had to ask him to leave for his unkind comments to his wife and child. This was totally unacceptable behavior he would not allow. Several days later the troubled friend called and apologized. The chaplain wants me to make a copy of "Are You an Answered Prayer" devotion to put in his hand to take with him to prison to read for encouragement. He wants to show him the chaplain IS that kind of friend for him. The chaplain obeys the word for it says in 2 Timothy 4:2 "Preach the Word; be prepared in season and out of season: correct, rebuke, and encourage-with great patience and careful instruction." This chaplain has witnessed to me about correcting, rebuking, and yet being encouraging. Wow! That would be difficult to do in this case but God has empowered him to do that. As for me I am amazed as to what God is going to do through these devotions in your life and mine. 2 Peter 3:9 "The Lord is not slow in keeping his promise, as some understand slowness. He is patient with you, not wanting anyone to perish, but everyone to come to repentance." The chaplain's patience is the same patience the Lord has with us and I believe he will use these devotions to bring me, you, and others to repentance. I should never underestimate God's power to use each of us- me writing devotions, the chaplain's patient encouragement, and who knows how he is going to use YOU. But I do know this: It will be good!

Yes, I am in the dating scene and no, this isn't what I would have chosen for myself, but I am here. You are going to meet people you wish you could have a relationship with and others you would like to avoid having a relationship with. That old saying of "Treat other people as you would like to be treated" is true. I am not suggesting you go out with people who are not good for you but to humble yourself a little bit and extend a little grace and mercy to some of the ones you are not attracted to. For instance, if you are at a dance what will it hurt you to dance occasionally with this person? Don't rob them of their dignity by letting them feel lesser than you. Romans 12:10 "Love one another with mutual affection, outdo one another in showing honor." Carry on a conversation with someone you find undesirable and some of that same honor may be extended back to you someday when you are that person who is not desired by someone you are interested in. 1 Peter 2:17 "Show proper respect to everyone: love the neighborhood of believers, fear God, honor the King" And Philippians 2:3-5 "Do nothing out of selfish ambition or vain conceit, but in humility consider others better than yourselves. Each of you should look not only to your own interests, but also to the interests of others. Your attitude should be the same as that of Christ Jesus." No one said humility was easy, but life isn't about you anyway. Love on others-you'll be glad you did.

Be the Best You Can Be

1 Corinthians 6:19-20 "Do you not know that your body is a temple of the Holy Spirit, who is in you, whom you have received from God? You are not your own; you were bought at a price. Therefore honor God with your body." I guess the point in this scripture has eluded me before or maybe I was trying to avoid the truth in it. The best reason for taking care of my body is whenever I do something bad to my body it would be like doing that to the Holy Spirit because He lives in me. The Holy Spirit is a gift God has given me. And on the other hand whenever I do something good for my body it would be a sweet offering to Christ as well. I am not my own. When I exercise and diet I am not just doing that for myself I do it because it is pleasing and honors God. Say "yes" to staying in shape. Say "no" to overeating and addictions to drinking, smoking, drugs, or anything that is not good for you. Say "yes" to your self-esteem as God empowers you with self-confidence because you reap the benefits of looking and feeling good. A temple is a special, Holy place just as your body is the house where God lives. It makes me want to look my best and act my best for him. The benefits are that others respect you for seeing the outward benefits of Christ in you and you will look great for that next special person in your life. Obey God's commands and He will reward you physically, spiritually, and emotionally. Take care of your temple and be the best you can be.

Galatians 6:10 "As we have opportunity, let us do good to all people."
Four years ago I was visiting at a church service with my friend. The
minister preached about God putting someone in your life and loving on
them. Before the close of the service I prayed that God would put
someone in our path. He didn't waste any time answering that prayer
because on our way to Sunday dinner with his family we found a man
hitchhiking out on a country road. My friend pulled over and offered him
a ride in the back of the pick up. The hitchhiker gladly jumped in with
what little belongings he had in a grocery bag. We took him to the
crossroads he asked for but my friend insisted on taking him all the way
to his destination. When we got there my friend said, "Man, it looks like
you've been through some hard times. Take this $20 and my business
card and call me if I can take you to church with me next Sunday." The
man wept. He thanked my friend and told us that this was his mom's
house and his stepdad would not want him to be there. The hiker was
down and out on his luck. A drug addiction cost him his marriage and
lastly his daughter left him too as he was evicted from the motel room
they were living in just the day before. He had no where to go and spent
the cold, winter night cuddled up under a bush at a nearby T.V. station
just trying to stay warm. He realized he should have died during the night
but God spared his life and now this act of kindness was evidence that
God loved him enough to put Godly people in his path.

He did have a desire to get back into church because my friend's
cell phone rang during lunch. It was our new friend saying please take
him to church that night. He couldn't wait until next Sunday. We quickly
changed our other plans and picked him up for Sunday night service. We
were amazed that the same man could make such a drastic change in his
appearance. He had showered, shaved and had on some clean clothes
with jeans that were now too large for him. My friend took of his belt
and offered it to him to wear. We went to church and worshipped in a
new light of a person crying out praises to God and hanging on to every
word the minister said. He went down at the altar call and rededicated his
life to Christ. My friend went down to join him in support and then came
back to the pew teary eyed. God had allowed us to be a part of this. I was
impressed with how others at church loved on this man too.

As time passed my friend helped the new friend get a job,
purchased some tools for him, and tried to get him enrolled in a drug
rehabilitation program. I kept in touch with my friend to check up on the
new convert. We lost touch eventually with our new friend as problems
persisted for him, but I am still reminded to pray often for the hitchhiker.
Who knows what God is doing in his life right now, but I do know I
witnessed God's love in action through my friend's going the second
mile with his compassion for a man who needed a little love at the time. I

dedicate this devotion to him as I pray it will inspire many others to go and do likewise. My sweet friend this is your scripture: Matthew 24:46 "When the master comes and finds the servant doing his work, the servant will be blessed." I pray blessings on you today. And for our struggling hitchhiker: 2 Corinthians 3:18 "And as the Spirit of the Lord works within us, we become more and more like him." I am praying the Holy Spirit will continue to work in your heart to create you to be the complete man God has called you to be. I pray you will pass the same love given to you on to others as it was given to you. God will use your struggles to strengthen you in helping someone else one day. God bless!

My youngest son when he was about seven expressed his concern to me about divorce because a playmate of his was going through that at the time. I assured him he would never have to worry about that. Some ten years later he WAS dealing with that. Some things just wrench your heart out. Try as hard as I could I could not save the marriage I saw deteriorating before my very eyes. I believe the human side of us wants to take responsibility for things we said in our lives and beat ourselves up about it. All of you reading this understand how important a cohesive family unit is to your child's well being and development no matter how old your children are when the storm of divorce comes along. God reassures us in Isaiah 43:18-19 "Forget the former things; do not dwell on the past. See, I am doing a new thing. Now it springs up; do you not perceive it? I am making a way in the desert and streams in the wasteland." This springing up is the peace and contentment you feel given to you by the Holy Spirit as He guides you through the deserts and wastelands of divorce in your family with streams of provision which God uses to heal you and your broken children. God is saying "Look up" as he told Abram in Genesis13:v14 "Lift up your eyes from where you are and look north, and south and east and west. V.15 All the land that you see I will give to you and your offspring forever. V.17…for I am giving it to you." Don't look down and beat yourself up for that is not God. Look up and forward and out at what God has promised for you and your children. Don't B-E-A-T yourself up but B-E up!

I believe that if it is your heart's desire to marry again God will grant you the desires of your heart. Matthew 6:33 "Seek ye first the kingdom of God and all these things will be added unto you." Consider this to be your time of training with God to be a better spouse the next time. Get in the word and learn from Christ's example on how to love. Ask God to teach you to love others as much as Christ loved the church. It will strengthen all of your relationships. Love and Jesus Christ are synonymous. How great is your God that he would reveal the most precious gift He has through Jesus Christ and share Him with us to allow the Holy Spirit to live in us, guide us, direct us, and nurture us in to becoming the best possible person we can be? Others will benefit from our love and share back what we give to them. Philippians 4:19 "And my God will meet all your needs according to his glorious riches in Christ Jesus." I don't know about you but I am hanging on to God's promise that He will meet <u>ALL</u> my needs. I want to marry again and I want to do it better the next time. That is one of the greatest riches in Christ Jesus is to make us better and better by giving us the Christlike way to love in all of our relationships. God is a God of second chances and He will give you the opportunity to love again.

Complete Me

Philippians 1:6 "He who began a good work in you will carry it on to completion until the day of Christ Jesus." Thank the Good Lord that He will not give up on me until I am complete. Taking each day one step at a time and not worrying about tomorrow gets us one step closer to who Jesus wants us to be. One of the Satan attacks used against me in singleness is to worry not so much about the past but uncertainties about the future. Will I have to spend the rest of my days alone? Will I have financial stability to make ends meet on my own? Will I spend my dying days as I have seen others do in nursing homes all alone with no one to care? Can you relate or is it just me? The assurances I receive come from God. If I get distressed or anxious I meditate on His word. Matthew 6:27 "My worrying and being anxious will not add one unit of measure to my stature or to the span of my life." (AMP) and Mark4:19 (NIV) "I will not let the worries of this life, the deceitfulness of wealth and the desires for other things come in and choke the word, making it unfruitful." God promises in His word He will give me what I need when I need it. "I will not worry and be anxious saying, What am I going to eat, or what am I going to drink, or what am I going to wear… But I will seek (aim at and strive after) first of all His Kingdom and His righteousness (His way of doing and being right), and then all these things taken together will be given me besides." Matthew 6:31,33 (AMP) I am a work in progress and I plan to seek first of all His kingdom. My worries will fade away because of His strength in me and God will carry me on until I am complete without worry and concern. Thank you for carrying me to completion.

Crying Out to God

A friend called and gave me some scriptures telling me I needed to cry out to God. 1 Samuel 7:8-9 the Israelites said to Samuel, "Do not stop crying out to the Lord our God for us, that he may rescue us from the hand of the Philistines…He cried out to the Lord on Israel's behalf, and the Lord answered him." Psalm 34:15, 17-18 "The eyes of the Lord are on the righteous and his ears are attentive to their cry. The righteous cry out, and the Lord hears them; he delivers them from all their troubles. The Lord is close to the brokenhearted and saves those who are crushed in spirit." and 1 Samuel 1:1-10 tells of Hannah as she cries out to God for a child. V. 10 "In bitterness of soul Hannah wept much and prayed to the Lord" v.15 "I am a woman who is deeply troubled, I have not been drinking wine or beer, I was pouring out my soul to the Lord" v. 20 "So in the course of time Hannah conceived and gave birth to a son . She named him Samuel, saying, 'Because I asked the Lord for him.' "

When you get to the deepest pit of despair cry out to God. A Christmas Eve I will never forget was when my son's wife left him. He was at home alone in another town and calling me. He was an emotional wreck and was begging me to come get him. I could not drive due to a recent surgery. I was not clearheaded enough to make the trip and had all ready had a wreck in my car when I stubbornly took myself to the grocery store before time to drive. I knew I could not go and in anguish I did not know where to turn. I knew he needed to be at home with his family and not alone. I called his father and he asked what did I want him to do about it. I asked him to go the three-hour drive to pick our son up and bring him to me. I explained I could not drive. I had not even talked to his father in over a year but I knew we were responsible for our son. In my frustration I got off the phone before I said something I would regret. I went outside, fell on my knees, and cried out to God to help because there was nothing I could do. I was on the driveway with hands uplifted and crying out to God. He heard my pleas for help because when I went inside the phone rang and it was my ex- husband saying he had decided to go get our son. I praised God for that. Six hours later my son was home and I nearly knocked him down with my hugs. God had provided by bringing my son safely home. We spent almost all night talking about his marriage successes and failures and mine as well.. It was obvious the marriage was over. He needed to talk and I needed to listen. Crying out to God? David said in Psalm 34:17-18 "The righteous cry out and the Lord hears them; He delivers them from all their troubles. The Lord is close to the brokenhearted and saves those who are crushed in spirit." Don't rely on your own strength. Cry out to Him. Cry out!

Dating temptations

In Daniel Chapter 1 Daniel is being trained for King Nebuchadnezzar to be the best possible he can be for the king's service. "The king assigned them a daily amount of food and wine from the king's table." Not just any food- the best food and wine for it was from the king's table. But Daniel resolved not to partake of this food and wine but to eat only vegetables and drink water for ten days as a sacrifice to prove his obedience to God. At the end of ten days he looked healthier and better than any of the young men who ate the royal food.

Who is it you are seeing in a relationship right now? Is this person of the world and like the king's dishes of fine foods, meats, sauces, and toppings that are so tantalizing and appealing? I love food so much I could really relate to Daniel's temptation to eat those worldly foods of the king and to drink wine that could give me temporary happiness and giddiness. Is that person like that to you? What I see in this example shown by Daniel's faith was he trusted in God's plan and he was healthier and stronger than following man's plan. Wait for God's provision for you. Resist the temptations. Jeremiah 29:11 "For I know the plans I have for you plans to prosper you and not to harm you, plans to give you hope and a future." Your plans or God's plan? The creator knows what is best for you. As a result you will be the best possible you can be for our King's service.

Deception in Dating

It is difficult to find someone to date who is honest to you about themselves, their past, and their present. Internet dating is tricky because people submit old photos of themselves to appear younger or in better shape. Sometimes when you're lined up with a date from a friend the blind date may even say things they know you want to hear from the information they have found out about you. When you feel comfortable enough with your date to ask about their past marriage they may even lie to you about how it ended to save face. A person who lies is usually pretty good at it because they have had much practice in it. You think you could see it in their face but not always.

Look for scriptures on truth and ask God who is the "God of truth" to reveal truths to you.

Jeremiah 33:3 "Call to me and I will answer you, and show you great and mighty things which you do not know."

Psalm 25:4-5 "Show me your ways, O Lord, teach me your path; guide me in your truth and teach me, for you are God my Savior, and my hope is in you all day long."

John 16:13 "But when He, the Spirit of truth comes, He will guide you into all truth."

Pray over these scriptures and claim them. You will be amazed at how quickly God will reveal truths to you about the person you are dating. Don't be deceived be relieved!

Delight in the Lord

I was just reading scriptures in the Bible and got so excited because I realize how they are for me and for you. They are not just words recorded on a page as annals in history. They are living, breathing, life giving words which you can claim for yourself. Read and insert your name or the names of loved ones you are praying for and listen to those words pop off that page into your heart and soul and mind. Putting faith and belief into the words of the living God brings life to you. It changes your whole perspective on reading the Word.

I am smiling and clapping with glee as I claim Psalm 1:1-3 "Blessed is the man who does not walk in the counsel of the wicked or stand in the way of sinners or sit in the seat of mockers. But his delight is in the law of the Lord, and on his law he meditates day and night. He is like a tree planted by streams of water, which yields its fruit in season and whose leaf does not wither. Whatever he does prospers." I don't know about you but I want to be blessed. I am delighting in the Word of God as God lays claim on me and promises to satiate my desires with eternal, living water which will allow me to flourish and not wither. Most importantly, whatever I do will prosper. Believe the word of God, claim it for yourself and the end result is you will desire to meditate on God's word day and night. Claim Matthew 11:11 "I tell you the truth: Among those born of women there has not risen anyone greater than John the Baptist (substitute in your name.)" Believe it, claim it, delight in it because God loves you that much. Delight in the Lord and He will Delight in you!

Denial or Acceptance?

Pilate saw no charge against Jesus but the Jews and Chief priests wanted Jesus crucified. Pilate asked John 19:15 "Shall I crucify your king?" The chief priests answered, "We have no king but Caesar." John 19:17 What about us? Why do we not claim Jesus' kingship over us? Why do we deny He is Lord over all we are and all we own? We are nothing without Him. Is He so small that He cannot take us through this experience in our lives? Do we doubt His kinship over our every day of existence?

I don't know where I have been in my faith walk all through the years of my life, but I am finally clearly seeing God in each part of my life that before I felt was just coincidence, chance, or just every day occurrences. It is healthy to look back over your life and recount specific events, people brought into your life, situations where God protected you , and decisions He led you to make. This is an act of praise to God when we give all the glory to Him. Acts 3:25 "And you are heirs of the prophets and of the covenant God made with your fathers. He said to Abraham 'Through your offspring all peoples on earth will be blessed.' " God all ready has blessed us when He sent Jesus to be King. Not just some ….All will be blessed. Claim and accept your inheritance as heirs to a king who rules supremely over our lives.

This morning I saw I had missed a 3:45 AM call from my mother. Thoughts raced through my head. My mom had called to tell me my brother who lives alone was extremely sick and had called an ambulance to go to the hospital. Everything is okay with the proper medication for him, but it certainly made me think about how transitory and fleeting this life is. We take for granted what difference one phone call in our lives could make. I love my brother dearly and it made me think about how important relationships are.

God put on my heart to think about relationships and loving that person as though it was the last day with them. Galatians 5:13... "serve one another in love." Romans 12:10 "Love one another with mutual affection; outdo one another in showing honor." Don't miss out on a chance to show someone you love then and just how much they mean to you. I have heard countless, sad stories about how someone died and a person missed a chance to put aside a grudge, or hurt, or just tell them how much they cared. Tell me-what regrets can you have in doing the right thing? The gain by understanding the cost of a potential loss can make you appreciate each day with that person much more. As the old song lyrics say "Every day with you is sweeter than the day before. Every day I love you more and more, more and more and more. And when I go to sleep at night time you're the one I'm praying for. For every day with you is sweeter than the day, sweeter than the day, sweeter than the day before." Don't suffer loss in order to appreciate the gain you have in a special relationship in your life. Don't delay. Act on it today!

My Treasure is You

After you have suffered a tremendous loss like divorce it opens your eyes to look at all things with a renewed perspective on their value. When my son also experienced divorce I told him to find joy in the small things like the sensation of the hot water in a shower, the beauty of a small flower, a sunset's beautiful colors, or the relationships you have with family and friends. Because of this new appreciation for everything relationships reach a new level of importance. It hurts to the very core of my heart when I hear my married friends speak harshly to one another or put each other down. I think how could they possibly do that? Don't they know or appreciate what they have in each other? Proverbs 3:13-15 (NKJV) "Happy is the man who finds wisdom, and the man who gains understanding; for her proceeds are better then the profits of silver, and her gain than fine gold. She is more precious than rubies, and all the things you may desire cannot compare with her." I pray that you never have to lose something to appreciate what you have. I pray God will give you wisdom and understanding to see your family, church, and work relationships are so important. These relationships are better than silver, gold, and any jewels of the world. Let God reveal to you what is important in life so that you will never waste a single day taking someone dear to you for granted. Silver, gold, rubies….No thanks, I'll take the wisdom God offers to show me the treasures I all ready have like YOU!

For Better or Worse

Recently I reread the marriage vows I had spoken many years ago and saw "for better or worse." God has been there for me as my marriage partner since the divorce through good and bad times. My divorce counselor gave me this scripture early on- Isaiah 54:5-7 "For your maker is your husband-the Lord Almighty is his name- the Holy One of Israel is your Redeemer; he is called the God of all the earth." (How could I possibly think my needs will not be met when I have the God of all the earth taking care of me?) "The Lord will call you back as if you were a wife deserted and distressed in spirit" (are these scriptures written just for me? I was deserted and I was distressed in Spirit) "a wife who married young only to be rejected, says your God" (rejected due to an affair my husband had with another woman) "for a brief moment, I abandoned you, but with deep compassion I will bring you back." (You have brought me back!) I have seen weekends with nothing planned and no one to do plans with, stormy nights, and lonely days, but I have not been alone because God was with me through it all. "For better or worse." I'd say it has been an experience of give and take mostly where I have been given to and God has unfolded layers and layers to reveal who I am in Christ. "For better or worse" in this relationship has definitely been for better. Thank you, Lord, for being my husband.

New Look

Since I was five years old I have been traveling over a dam at Lake Murray from my grandmother's house to a lake cottage we inherited. My grandmother has long passed away but I still travel this familiar route because my parents bought a house on the same side of town. As I cross the dam I see a beautiful view of wide open expanse of lake with blue waters and dark green treelines in the distance. Every time we crossed that lake I looked at the views. Recently the dam was renovated from earthen to concrete and a nice walking path was added for people needing exercise. A friend accompanied me on a walk there one evening and asked me to tell how many towers there were for the power company in the water just off the dam, but with one stipulation- I couldn't look. I guessed four and was wrong. There are five. Isn't it amazing that all these years of traveling over this dam and I couldn't tell you how many towers in the water?

It made me think about my reading the Bible. All these years I have been reading the Bible and God is calling me to look at the scriptures with a fresh eye as if I have never seen it before. He is trying to allow new details and insights for me which are God revealed. Jeremiah 23:29 "Is not my word like fire, declared the Lord, and like a hammer that breaks a rock in pieces." Break me into pieces so that the Word is like fire burning into my soul, Lord. Matthew 4:4 "Jesus answered, It is written, 'Man does not live on bread alone, but on every word that comes from the mouth of God.' " Feed me, sustain me with your holy words. And Col.3:16 "Let the word of Christ dwell in you richly…" Have the word dwell in me, Lord. Open the eyes of my heart to see you more clearly. Don't let me overlook the details important to my life. Continue to cause me to look with newness on every word. Amen.

Remain in Love

Have you been through one divorce or more? Has someone significant walked out on you? Has rejection just been the theme of your life from childhood? Did a parent not know how to show you the love you needed? Have you had a series of broken relationships with romantic encounters, family members, and worse yet your own children? The worst thing Satan can do to you is to build up a wall around your heart. You have been hurt so many times your heart is calloused to pain. It is not good when your heart becomes hardened. It is God's desire that we love each other. John 15:17 "This is my command: Love each other." Don't be so disappointed about these relationships. I once heard people are put in your life for a reason a season, or forever. Love again even though you were hurt before. John 15:9-10 "As the Father has loved me so have I loved you. Now remain in my love. If you obey my commands, you will remain in my love, just as I have obeyed my Father's commands and remain in his love." What could be better than this than to REMAIN in Jesus's love for us and have our Father's love as well. I like that word remain because fleeting would be a word to describe my past earthly relationships. Yours too! We need the permanency of Jesus-remain in His love. John 15 continues on in verses 11 and 12 "I have told you this so that my joy may be in you and that your joy may be complete. My command is this. Love each other as I have loved you." How do you find joy? Continue to love each other. People may have been put in your life for a reason or season but Jesus is put in your life forever. Remain with your love, Lord, so my joy will be complete.

"There is no situation so chaotic that God cannot, from that situation, create something that is surpassingly good. He did it at the creation. He did it at the cross. He is doing it today." Bishop Moule

As you read this I pray that you will receive the blessing from it. The hurt of loneliness, rejection, and defeat can be so great that your heart aches with pangs that physically feel like a heart attack. Hang on, trust and obey God for something far greater than we can think or imagine is going to come form this situation if you will just let God have His way in your heart. Perhaps from your suffering you can share some time with someone else who is hurting. Listen to their story and pray for their healing. You know this scripture to be true: "A word in due season can lighten a friend's load" Proverbs 15:23 because it has happened to you. A phone call came just when you were hurting most, a hug from a friend, a card in the mail, or a gladness of heart you just can't explain other than God's mercy and grace. Take the focus off of your valleys so that God will allow you to "See" the need in others and provide you with opportunities to walk with them through their trials from their valleys to the sea. A sea open with possibilities for their future. A sea with a sense of expectation and joy because their God is with them and He sent a friend who cares for them.

Romans 12:1-2 "Therefore, I urge you, brothers, in view of God's mercy, to offer your bodies as living sacrifices, holy and pleasing to God-this is your spiritual act of worship. Do not conform any longer to the pattern of this world, but be transformed by the renewing of your mind. Then you will be able to test and approve what God's will is-his good, pleasing and perfect will." Once you have been married and enjoyed intimacy with a partner it is very difficult to give it up. Sometimes I have lain in bed at night and prayed that God would take that desire away from me for now because it causes my heart to ache and a void is in my life of unfulfilled desires. Talking with other divorced women I have found they struggle with the same thing. Some have just followed their desires in relationships and just ended up even more broken and hurt by the void. Paul in Romans encourages us to offer our bodies as living sacrifices…this is our spiritual act of worship. I have found an accountability partner and we openly discuss and hold each other accountable in our dating and serious relationships. It is great to have someone who understands and is going through the same struggles. She prays for me and calls with a scripture or devotion that is always right on time when I need it. She in turn shares her struggles as we ask for God to give us the strength to not conform to the pattern of this world but to renew our mind and transform us into that living and holy sacrifice which is pleasing to God. God knows what is best for us and waiting for intimacy in marriage is what is best. Find a friend to support you and wait for God's direction to show you his good, pleasing, and perfect will. Just meditate on those words, good, pleasing, and perfect. Those are the promises God gives you to follow after His heart not ours. I don't know about you but my heart has been broken enough. Do I want to follow God's plan, My plan of brokenness, or God's plan of fulfillment?

Trust and Obey

When my husband left me during the Christmas holidays I thought my world was falling apart. Exercise makes me feel better so I decided to go for a run. I run trails in the woods and a vivid memory was when I fell to my knees out in the woods and just cried out to the Lord for help. I was broken and could not do it on my own. The voice in my head said "Trust and Obey." That has been my motto through this whole divorce, "Trust and Obey." Mind you, I didn't say it was easy. Trusting in God is a daily renewal process. We arrogant humans think we can do this our own way. How many times has God shown us that we can't? Or we give the problem to Him and take it back. We give it to Him and take it back. Proverbs 3:5-6 "Trust in the Lord with all your heart and lean not on your own understanding. In all your ways acknowledge Him and He will make your path straight." Sometimes you have to trust God enough to give up on the relationship and just move on with your life. "See I am doing a new thing." Isaiah 43:19. It has been five years now of singleness and God reassures me over and over again that He is there every step of the way. Allow Him to do that in your life and He will fulfill His promises by "making your paths straight." I am so much happier when He directs my path instead of me guiding my path.

Give in order to Receive

2 Corinthians 9:6 "Remember this: Whoever sows sparingly will also reap sparingly, and whoever sows generously will also reap generously." Many injustices have been against you in your life: Loss of job, loss of relationship, physical pain through illness, broken relationships with your very own children. These could be some of the things you have suffered. But are you able to forgive the persons involved in these circumstances and even God for allowing it to happen? I always thought sowing meant giving of money to others but I believe it is more than that. Because of all the hurt and loss you have suffered in your past are you closing off your heart to love? I believe love is a type of sowing, as well. Try inserting these words into the scripture. "Whoever forgives sparingly will also be forgiven sparingly and whoever forgives generously will also be forgiven generously." Insert love in there. "Whoever loves sparingly will also be loved sparingly and whoever loves generously will also be loved generously." Yes, give in order to receive. This human walk is difficult. We must forgive when we don't want to and we must love when we don't want to, but God promises to give back generously to you what you sow into others. We must forgive in order to be forgiven. We must love in order to be loved. Sowing is the small effort for the bounty or reaping we will receive. After all God says "generously." The returns are far greater than the cost. Psalm 138:8 "The Lord will fulfill his purpose for me"even though I find it difficult to forgive and love. Your love, O God endured forever and will see me through these times of sowing and reaping. Teach me to sow in order to reap your blessings, O God. Teach me to give so that I may receive your love and forgiveness.

Want to know how to love? Forgive. God will forgive you for much which opens the door for you to love much. It helps me to understand people who shut themselves off from love. Unless they are able to forgive they are limited in how much they can love. Luke 7:47 "Therefore, I tell you, her many sins have been forgiven-for she loved much. But he who has been forgiven little loves little." Listen to the person you are dating and if they sound very bitter about their past then their capacity to love is limited. Also, I think it is important for us to humble ourselves and ask God for forgiveness. If you can admit to mistakes you have made in relationships rather than always being right about everything then you can humble yourself and grow. Allow God to work as a loving father in your life to show you his guidance and direction to mold you into a better person. "But he who has been forgiven little loves little." Little equals little. Forgiving large equals loving large. God has allowed many opportunities of forgiveness in my life: an ex-husband's affair with the woman he married, a broken nose from a student's anger, hurtful words spoken, broken dating relationships, hateful deeds performed by a neighbor and the list goes on as it does for you. God has taken me to a place of forgiveness for each of these offenses and taught me to pray for the offender. A sweet release came to me when I did this. Matt. 6:14-15 "For if you forgive men when they sin against you, your heavenly Father will also forgive your sins. But if you do not forgive men their sins, your Father will not forgive your sins." Think how freeing it is to forgive. How can you do otherwise? Give in order to receive forgiveness. Love in order to receive love.

John 10:4… "and his sheep follow him because they know his voice." Countless times God has spoken to me to reveal things. My father had dementia and his health had been declining for many years. One morning getting ready for work God told me I needed to go home. I called work and told them I wouldn't be there that day. I drove the hour and a half trip home. My mother was exhausted from being the care giver. I spent time alone with Dad telling him what a good father, husband, minister, and man he had been and gave him permission to go on and be with the Lord. He died about thirty minutes later. Did he understand what I said? I believe he did. He had fought the good fight and it was time to go. How do you explain that I knew to be there that very day? I can explain it. God speaks to us and reveals things to us. "Call to me and I will answer you and show you great and mighty things which you did not know." Jeremiah 33:3 I wouldn't give anything for those last moments with my dad. God is good to reveal special things to us. I pray that we stay connected to God by spending time with him so that we will recognize his voice when the good shepherd speaks to us. John 10:3 "The watch man opens the gate for him, and the sheep listen to his voice. He calls his own sheep by name and leads them out." Lead me, God, Lead me.

Silent Sons, Speaking Father

I have two adult sons in their twenties. One tells me what is going on in his life some of the time and the other never tells me what is going on. Two weeks elapsed before I found out the oldest had broken his collar bone in a severe motorcycle crash. And the only way I found that out was when I went to visit my out of town sons. When I got there he had his arm in a sling. His motorcycle was pretty much destroyed. He said it would take 24 hours to tell the whole story. I told him I was probably better off not knowing. He agreed because he realizes this is the second crash which has been near fatal. The details of the first crash was enough to make any Mother grayheaded for life.

I pray for both sons daily, the one who shares and the one who does not. And the one who shares at times is the one who waited two weeks to let me know about the crash. So you realize how tough is it to get any information from the youngest. At times our conversations last three minutes with his one word yes or no answers to my questions. I think you can sense my frustration as I can probably relate to yours with your children. Daily prayer for them is how I cope because whether I know the details or not God knows even their thoughts in their heads even before they think it. It is reassuring to abide in His rest knowing He has my children's best interests at heart. A friend shared a scripture with me about not turning from your own, but always consider their needs. Isaiah 58:7-9 "Is it not to share your food with the hungry and to provide the poor wanderer with shelter-when you see the naked to clothe him, and not to turn away from your own flesh and blood? Then your light will break forth like the dawn, and your healing will quickly appear; then your righteousness will go before you, and the glory of the Lord will be your rear guard. Then you will call, and the Lord will answer; you will cry for help, and he will say; Here am I."

This helps me to know my prayers are being answered for my sons because the Lord is my rear guard and theirs. When I call out to the Lord He will be right there with them and with me to give me what to pray about. I am claiming the scripture Jeremiah 33:3 "Call to me and I will answer you and show you great and mighty things which you did not know." I am asking God to reveal to me what I am to be blanketing them in prayer about. I especially need God on days of danger and struggles for him to reveal to me so that I may not turn away from my own flesh and blood. It is only through God's supernatural strength that I am able to be the mother I need to be anyway. Tell it to me or not, boys, because God is my rear guard and He will show me when and what to pray. My sons are silent but my Father speaks. Thank you, Lord Jesus for empowering me to be a praying parent.

Difficult to Love

Difficult people in our lives are sometimes best understood if we can figure out where they are coming from. What past experiences in their lives did they have? What are their hurts and insecurities? My father came from some very unfortunate circumstances that helped me understand his moods. Forgiveness has to do with putting yourself in the other's shoes to some degree. A better word for it is to "empathize" with them. God will put it on your heart to pray for these difficult people in your life. Matthew 5:44-45 "Love your enemies and pray for those who persecute you, so that you may be children of your Father in heaven; for he makes his sun rise on the evil and on the good, and sends rain on the righteous and on the unrighteous." Once you pray for them it is easier to deal with them and to not allow them to have control over your emotions, but God will have control. Why did your spouse treat you the way he/she did? Try to understand his/her side of the situation and what events from their past led them to what happened. It will be a sweet release to you to understand them a little better, put it aside, and to be able to move on. Luke 6:37 (NKJV) "I condemn not, and I shall not be condemned. I forgive, and I will be forgiven." Condemning only condemns you. That is why when you forgive you feel a sweet release and peace comes over you. Forgiveness is necessary for difficult people and for you.

Little Thing or Big Thing

As a retired high school teacher I went back to fill in a maternity leave at a middle school. The middle school concept of staying on the same curriculum with all teachers testing on the same test for monitoring progress was a new concept to me. In giving a test I realized I had inadvertently left out two items when I zeroxed the pages. Those two were on the back side of a page which I had overlooked. I felt it was my error so I didn't penalize the students for the last two. I didn't realize giving them the answer to the last two items ended up skewing my results. At the next department meeting student responses were discussed in regards to areas of strengths and weaknesses. It wasn't until the end of the meeting that it clicked in my head that those two items I had given them were the ones they were bragging on. Rather than admit to it I kept my mouth shut and figured none would be the wiser. After all I didn't want these young, wise teachers to realize this old, veteran teacher could be losing her cutting edge. That afternoon on my drive home God convicted me by asking, "If I can't trust you with the little things how can I trust you with the big things?" That caused me to squirm about my little coverup. The next day I emailed my boss, the principal, the assistant principal and the other grade level teachers to explain my mistake and to apologize. It was tough to eat humble pie but I felt so much better. 1Timothy 4:12 "Set an example in speech in life, in love, in faith, and in purity." And another scripture "Let us not grow weary in doing what is right, for we will reap at harvest time, if we don not give up." Galatians 6:9 The question God asked me was could He trust me and the question I ask is did my witness make an impact on someone else? I hope so. As a result I pray God will be able to trust me with the bigger things. That would be the harvest I want to reap. Can God trust you with the little things?

Valleys or Mountaintops?

After reading about the Hall of Fame Bible greats in Hebrews 11:8-12 what I don't know is if they ever wavered in hope like I tend to do. I wonder if Jacob while he was imprisoned ever wondered how will I fulfill God's promise in here behind bars. Or did Satan attack Noah and say, "You fool, why did you build an ark when there is no such thing as rain?" Or did Sarah give up hope every once in a while when she saw wrinkles and gray hair? I wish I knew because I question God's promise to give me a spouse. Is my spouse ever going to come? I get so lonely and distraught at times usually after a big "God moment" where God allowed me to witness or pray for someone. After a weekend spiritual retreat or coming back home after a mission trip I feel down and lose hope. Not all of life is a spiritual mountaintop experience. The comfort I receive when I am let down is the word of God like this: 1 John 4:13-16 "We know that we live in Him and He in us, because he has given us of the Spirit. And we have seen and testify that the Father has sent his son to be the Savior of the world. If anyone acknowledges that Jesus is the Son of God, God lives in him and he in God. And so we rely on the love God has for us. God is love. Whoever lives in love lives in God and God in him." What more reassurance do I need when I get melancholy? God is love and He lives in me. So what could I possibly have to worry about? Live in me, God, and me in you. I want to rely on the love YOU have for me!

Distraction or Attraction?

I have seen so many of my friends in their loneliness and despair keep them- selves busy so as to fill their schedules. This busyness keeps them from being lonely. A busy day at work, sports, dinners out, dancing, activities and activities and activities. The television becomes that for us too as we turn on the television so that we can get "lost" in what we see. Is this distraction helpful? Perhaps at times, but God wants our focus and attention on Him so that we can get out of neutral, spinning our wheels, and moving forward to Drive where we heal and move on with our lives.

Philippians 4:19 "And my God will meet all your needs, according to his glorious riches in Christ Jesus." Who will meet your needs? God will. Which of your needs will God meet? **All** of your needs. He won't just meet your needs He will meet all your needs with riches in Christ Jesus. Seek God to meet your needs not television, activities, or people. None of those can meet your needs. Allow yourself quiet time with just you and the Lord. Allow yourself times of love with Him. He has so many riches and blessings He wants to give you. Bask in the one true love who doesn't disappoint-God. Your attraction to Him will only bring rewards.

Divorce Singleness-Apart from family?

Have you been concerned about divorce splitting up a family or singleness with no family of your own? I'm sure we have all tried to reason through this at one time or another. Why me? Why am I still alone? Why do my children have to leave me or go spend time with their mom or dad? What about the family unit?

In these times God is with you through it all. He loves you more than the numbers of all the grains of sand on the whole earth. Is that hard to conceive or to be able to wrap your thoughts around? How about He knows how many hairs are on your head? What about you are <u>never</u> off of His mind? When you can just begin to comprehend how much He loves you then all of our circumstances become a little more bearable. In the Bible He even refers to you as son or daughter and He wants you to refer to Him as father.

As you read in the Bible, pay attention to the concept of family, of a father who loves you as the scriptures use son, daughter, child of God, Jesus and God as our father.

Proverbs 2:1 "My <u>son,</u> if you accept my words…"

Matthew 6:9 "Our <u>father</u> in heaven…"

Matthew 5:9 "Blessed are the peacemakers, for they will be called <u>sons</u> of God."

Lamentations 2:13 "<u>Daughter</u> of Jerusalem, Daughter of Zion"

Matthew 12:50 "for whoever does the will of my Father in heaven is my <u>brother and sister and mother.</u>"

Do you feel special? You should. If you believe Jesus Christ died on the cross to save you from your sins, you confess, and repent then You are a part of the royal family, the best conceivable family- God's.

Independence with God

One of the most devastating things I have ever had to happen in my life was for my husband of 24 years to willingly choose someone else over me. My feelings of self-worth plummeted. I went through a period of deep depression in those last struggling years we were together. I knew the affair was going on but could never quite prove it. When I couldn't prove anything but went on hunches and heard the lies I even suspected my own sanity. The disguise of what was a pretense of marriage was wearing me down. Work was beginning to be a haven, a place away from the realities at home. Sensing something was not quite right my children had a warring spirit. Yet through all of this my faith walk was growing. God was guiding me with His strength to face the future.

How do you grow in independence? By being in dependence on God. Hebrews 4:16 "Let us approach the throne of grace with confidence, so that we may receive mercy and find grace to help us in our time of need." Step by step God has led me, shown me, and grown me into a lady of confidence and self-worth. I walk into a room now with my head held high. Why? Because Psalm 30:2 "I cry out to the Lord and He heals me." Luke 2:40 (AMP) "I am growing and becoming strong in spirit, filled with wisdom; and the grace (favor and spiritual blessing) of God is upon me." As I have drawn closer to God He has drawn closer to me. That love is never taken away from you and fills you with a self-confidence and worth in God that no person can ever fill. How do you grow? Want to receive all the love you can possibly imagine? Live in dependence on God.

Do you trust God completely? Then turn all your hurts and disappointments over to Him and let him handle those feelings for you. Let God be the arbitrator and judge not Satan. As so many of your marriages ended due to an affair so did mine. I don't know how anyone survives that kind of brokenness without the Holy Spirit's indwelling in us. Seven years of an affair that went on and off during those painful years left me a broken woman with pieces which God picked up and put back together to make me whole. How can that be possible? God brought me to a place of forgiveness where I can now pray for my ex-husband and for his marriage with his wife with a heart of forgiveness which gives me the desire to pray that <u>they</u> have a happy and fulfilled marriage. Proverbs 25:21-22 "If your enemy is hungry, give him food to eat; if he is thirsty, give him water to drink. In doing this, you will heap burning coals on his head and the Lord will reward you." I don't want burning coals on their head. Instead I want the burning desire in me to fulfill God's purposes in my life. To do this, first, start praying for each person who has offended you. Then God will work in your heart to allow you to forgive. Through prayer he will mold your heart to have a genuine desire for what is best for <u>them</u> in their lives. The reward is I am walking forward in God's confidence in who I am as a free woman without the shackles of bitterness and hatred dragging me down. A friend once told me I could hold on to my bitterness and anger and drown or I could let it go and swim to the top.

God handles my inner struggles of anger, hatred, and bitterness. He fights those battles for me in the deepest whirlpools of human emotions and sets me free to swim to the top. Romans 12:21 says "Do not be overcome by evil, but overcome evil with good." That is the benefit God promises as your judge and arbitrator in Proverbs 25:22. "and God will reward you." Let God be the judge. He is the one seated at the throne and by giving Him the power to heal you in your life He sets you free to swim to the top. That is your reward. What a sweet, sweet freedom. Swim, my friend, swim.

Odd leads to Even

3....6....9.... the numbers associated with the time Jesus is placed on the cross. All or these are odd numbers. At hour 3 they crucified him. Hour 6 darkness came over the whole land. Hour 9 Jesus cried out, "My God, my God, why have you forsaken me?" Mark 15:34 and Jesus died. Three, six, nine odd numbers with very significant impact. How does the even come into play? The word even always has a positive connotation. Only good came from Christ dying on the cross. What good? Christ died for us even while we were yet sinners.

God can take the odd numbers in your life (addictions, abuses, divorces, neglect, hatred) and use these as your sacrifices. Turn them into something wonderful in your life when you minister to others. Hebrews 13:15-16 "Through Jesus, therefore let us continually offer to God a sacrifice (addictions, abuses, past hurts) of praise-the fruit of lips that confess his name. And do not forget to do good and to share with others, for with such sacrifices God is pleased." Proclaim your love for Jesus Christ for where he has brought you today despite these negatives in your past. Let the odds in your life turn to evens. Jesus was the best example of that 3, 6, 9. Let your odd numbers grow incrementally so that more and more praises to God can bring glory to God from the odds in your life. Odd leads to even.

Eagles' Wings

The scripture God has been giving me during my time of waiting on him to tell me what to do next in life about dating, buying a house, what job to take or not take, and what to do with my sons is Isaiah 40:31 "Those who wait for the Lord shall renew their strength. They shall mount up with the wings of eagles. They shall run and not grow weary. They shall walk and not faint." I hadn't noticed the reference to eagles in the Bible before but Exodus 19:4 states "You yourselves have seen what I did to Egypt, and how I carried you on eagles' wings and brought you to myself." The American symbol of majesty and power is the eagle. God referenced here in Exodus that he carried his people on eagles' wings above all earthly things closer to a heavenly realm where God is directing your flight in this journey. My mind visualizes flying high above the earth almost effortlessly with the power of the wind under my wings. My vision that was once blurred by worries is now like the eagle's. Just as an eagle's eye spots his prey so far away, as I fly I see clearly with God's focus. It is a glimpse of his splendor on even the smallest of His details in my life. My NIV translation of Isaiah 40:31... "Those who hope in the Lord will renew their strength. They will SOAR on wings like eagles." What I see in this is God carries you first when you don't know where to go. You are just allowing Him to carry you on eagles' wings and then by God's presence in your life, waiting, listening, and hoping in him he carries you to new heights where he empowers you to Soar on wings like eagles. God refreshes the weary and satisfies the faint. Thank you, Creator God , who created all the ends of the earth, all birds and earthly things that you give strength to the weary and power to the weak. When we cannot carry ourselves you carry us on eagles wings and teach us to get high enough to soar like eagles with your strength. Thank you for loving us like that. Amen.

Love Conquers All

My heart grieves when I hear Christians using condemning voices in reference to homosexuals, adulterers, drug abusers and others in sin. In the heat of a controversial issue our anger flares up. Why? Is it really that you care enough for that individual that you want the best for them or is it that there is some inherent anger at your own weaknesses and shortcomings which make you lash out at others? Ouch! Self-examination may reveal inner turmoil over some issue that allows you to strike out at others. I know you didn't want to hear that. I always hate it when I realize the flaw is in me not in someone else. The issue is sometimes what God needs to work out in your own heart. What does the approach of speaking in anger and condemnation accomplish anyway? Leviticus 19:18 "Do not seek revenge or bear a grudge against one of your people, but love your neighbor as yourself." If the deep-rooted problem is you can't even love yourself, then that emotion makes it easy to condemn others and difficult to love them. Jesus was the perfect example of loving others even through his times of suffering. He pleaded on the cross on our behalf, "Father, forgive them, for they do not know what they are doing." Yes, every time you speak in condemning tones about others you too helped drive that nail into the cross. Luke 23:34 If anyone deserved to condemn and lash out it was Jesus but he did not retaliate, He loved. That prayer is still for us today. We don't know what we are doing without the example of Jesus before us. The best way to make a difference is to admit we all have sinned and have no right to condemn. Choose Jesus's way to express a Christian love and concern for someone else. I believe the old saying "Love Conquers All" is true. If you really want to make a difference in the lives of homosexuals, adulterers, drug abusers and sinners like ourselves, extend love and mercy. Love the neighbor as yourself. Show them acts of kindness. This love works through God. Then instead of Love Conquers All "God Conquers All" because God is love.

"Home, home on the range where the deer and the antelope play where never is heard a discouraging word." Where never is heard a discouraging word. That evokes a sense of what "home" is like to all of us. "Where never is heard a discouraging word." How many times has someone offered up a word of encouragement to you at a time when you really needed it? I can't even count the number of times but I can certainly recall what sweet encouraging words were said to me and by whom. They go as far back as my childhood. Sweet, sweet memories are a blessing. Another blessing is to speak words of encouragement to others. They will listen to you because they know what you have been through and that YOU truly can empathize with them where they are right now. In Matthew 12 verses 34-35 Jesus said, "For out of the overflow to the heart the mouth speaks. The good man brings good things out of the good stored up in him, and the evil man brings evil things out of the evil stored up in him." I pray for you to have a wellspring of the heart for the overflow to spill out on others. A wellspring God allowed you to have. Why not share the blessing with others? Words from a well spring- a deep "well" supplied from living waters from God which "spring" out or flow to others. A spring that never runs dry for a lack of encouraging words. "Where never is heard a discouraging word."

Prescription for Healing

The Bible isn't just a book of historical events and recollections of past mistakes, it is a lifeline pertinent for today and for your situation and how to make things right. Would you like to be able to heal from your past and move on to the future? God gives the prescription for that in Isaiah 58: v.9 "If you do away with the yoke of oppression, with the pointing finger and malicious talk and if you spend yourselves in behalf of the hungry and satisfy the needs of the oppressed." (Quit complaining about our situation and placing blame on others for where you are. Instead take the focus off of yourself and help others who are hungry or oppressed.) If you do this then these six things will be your benefits.v. 10 then 1. "your light will rise in darkness 2. and your night will become like noonday v.11 3. The Lord will guide you always 4. he will satisfy your needs in a sun-scorched land 5.and He will strengthen your frame. You will be like a well-watered garden like a spring whose waters never fail 6.back up to v.8 Then your light will break forth like the dawn and your healing will quickly appear." The benefits far outweigh the sacrifice of time on your part to help. God will even open the doors for all the details to be worked out. Send cards of encouragement, pray for friends, text scriptures to others, go on a mission trip , volunteer with a charitable organization in your community, visit a shut in from your church or at the nursing home, be a mentor to a youth who has no father or no mother. The possibilities of service are endless as is the depth of those healing waters God will provide for you. After all he is the Doctor with the best prescription of healing. Follow His word and get well soon!

Matthew 13:43 "He who has ears let him hear." (I thought you just said heart and here we are talking about ears.) We need to use our ears to listen to what God is trying to teach us when it comes to matters of the heart. God says in Proverbs Chapter 4 verse 23 "Above all else, guard your heart, for it is the wellspring of life."

Do the lessons ever stop? I look back over my high school dating years and God definitely protected me. After the divorce getting back into that scene after so many years can truly be overwhelming. Maybe like me you are searching for someone to love because you have so much to share. I'll say I have probably fallen in love three times over the past five years of divorced life. That really hurts! Who do you cherish so much in life? I suspect in your case as in mine it is your children. Think about how you have treated them gently, molded them, shaped them into a complete full person so that now they are meeting their every need. So why would we treat something as precious as our heart any differently?

I am stronger now from past wrong love relationships but those "heart attacks" were because I didn't allow God into the heart of the matter. "Eye has not seen, nor ear heard, nor have entered into the heart of man the things which God has prepared for those who love Him." 1Corinthians 2:9 Listen to His words and let God lead and prepare your heart. Allow God to "guard" your heart. Listen to God with your ears to protect your heart.

Forgiveness
Pass It On

One of the richest blessings I ever received was a lesson on forgiveness. I am a part of a group of prayer intercessors for my city. For years we have been meeting twice a month to pray over concerns for leadership positions, local elections, schools, hospitals, emergency workers, churches, pastors, and even police matters. The sheriff is a Godly man and sought our help in praying for the unsolved murders in our city from the past twenty years. We went to a quadruple murder site to pray for God's will. The remaining family members came and as God would have it they witnessed to us more than the good we did for them. You and I cannot imagine what these families have been through. They have lost loved ones but there has been no closure because the murderers have not been apprehended. God took control of their lives and they shared briefly how He had been with them through it all. One family member met one of the other victim's family and they ended up getting married. What about that?! God took something Satan intended for evil and brought some good out of it. Late in the day after we prayed we went out to eat with the families. I was drawn to one particular couple who told their story of forgiveness and passing it on. The murder of their son put a stress on their marriage relationship which almost broke them apart. It was a long process to forgive whoever this murderer is but God brought them to that peace. Next, God stretched them to reach out to others suffering in the same way. They attended several meetings where victims' families met in a support group. They met the father of a girl who died in a hotel fire. The fire was the result of arson. His marriage did not survive the loss and he was all alone with the murder trial for the arsonist just days away. This couple took the time off from work to be with the bereaved father during the court sessions. They sat side by side with him. When the arsonist was brought into the courtroom rage filled the father of the victim. The understanding friend grabbed this father's hand and said, "What would Jesus do?" He was reminded of the scripture Luke 23:34 "Father, Forgive them, for they do not know what they are doing." The rage in the father melted to quiet tears as he thanked his friend for reminding him of that precious time Jesus forgave all, even us, of our sins. Tears were streaming down my face over my meal as I wondered about God's goodness to allow me to hear a testimony like that! Praise God from whom all blessings flow. Forgiveness? Yes, even you can forgive and assist someone else to see Christ's face as I saw it in this couple. Pass it on. Their face shines like Christ's face and so will yours.

Forgive by Example Part II

As I look back on valuable life lessons I have learned the most important was the one my father modeled for me on forgiveness. Ephesians 5:1 "Be imitators of God (or our Godly parents) therefore, as dearly loved children and live a life of love, just as Christ loved us…" My dad was left behind in Poland at an early age because he didn't have the proper immunization to come to the United States at the time his parents were coming. They thought it was best to leave him behind with an aunt as they went ahead to the promise of a new land and freedom. Several years later his parents sent for him to join them in New York. They had two other children during that time. Here was a new family which had been devoid of him. The emotional scars of being left behind followed him throughout his life. Not to mention he never completely felt a part of his family unit again. His mother disowned him when he accepted Christ at age 12 and he wanted to become a minister instead of a priest. His mother was a very strict Catholic. He was homeless at an early age. God had a design on his life though and worked all things out for good. A visiting Methodist minister came to learn from the sidewalk evangelist from whom Dad had heard the word of God preached on the busy street near Wall Street. Daddy Hall, the minister, introduced my dad to the visiting minister and it was all history from there. The young visiting minister took Daddy home and encouraged him to finish his schooling, go on to college, and seminary.

When I was 12, I insisted Daddy take me to New York to meet the grandmother I had never seen or even talked to. He scrimped and saved on a meager minister's salary and took me. I was excited when we got there. I ran up the driveway to hug my grandmother and she didn't respond at all. She just kept her arms down not returning the hug. We stayed a week and mealtime was especially painful because my grandmother acted as though my father wasn't even there. When we left I asked my daddy to never take me there again. Never once in my life did I hear him say anything that was derogatory about his mom. He only spoke of her in loving terms. With an example like that in life how could I do any less when my husband had an affair during seven years of our marriage, denied any part in it, and left me? It is because of my daddy's example that I still in part love my husband of 24 years through acts of mercy by never saying an unkind word about him. Jesus was the perfect example of forgiveness when He said, "Father, forgive them for they know not what they do." We on the other hand forgive because we Do Know what to do by the examples set before us on forgiveness. Who showed you forgiveness? Inherit forgiveness. Go and do likewise.

Sleepless Nights

Psalm 63:6 "When I remember thee upon my bed, and meditate on thee in the night watches." How many times have you fallen asleep and been awakened in the middle of the night not to fall asleep again? Or many times did you just toss and turn with seemingly no sleep at all?

This is another one of those great times to take the focus off of yourself to quiet your mind. Think about others who are in need and spend your time praying for them. Counting sheep just doesn't work but praying for them does.

Verse 7 gives some good advice-"Because you are my help, I sing in the shadow of your wings." Singing praise to God works! God doesn't care if you can sing or not, He just basks in your love for Him. If you are afraid you would wake up your spouse you can sing in your heart. Do you know that God knows your every thought? Then why not sing in your mind the praises to God? The comfort you receive comes from feeling Him close "in the shadow of His wings."

Verse 8 shows where our attention should be "My soul clings to you; your right hand upholds me." The reward is feeling His presence by His Holy Spirit in you. Before long you will be resting and abiding in Him.

1. Take the focus off yourself
2. Pray for others
3. Sing praises
4. Rest in God's presence

Psalm 62:5 "Find rest, O my soul, in God alone." Even a sleepless night can be a blessing when you find your rest in God alone.

Is there no man who
Is what he says he is?

I have found God to be a respecter of truths. Recently I have had things revealed to me in relationships which showed that person was lying. Has that happened to you as well? Since I have been praying that the God of truth would lead me in to all truths, lies have been exposed. So I question is there any man who is what he says he is?

The answer to that is clear. Yes, JESUS CHRIST IS WHO HE SAYS HE IS. That you can count on, rely on, depend on day in and day out now and through all eternity. Exodus 3:13-14... "and they ask me 'What is his name?' Then what shall I tell them?" God said to Moses, "I Am Who I Am, That is what you are to say to the Israelites, I Am has sent me to you." That I Am is everything your heart could ever dream or desire or want Him to be. Do you want love, care, kindness, thoughtfulness, patience, direction, provision for all your needs, and especially truthfulness? Whatever you need or desire He is I Am. As Jesus said in John 14:6 "I am the way the truth and the life." He is EVERYTHING you need. Man will always disappoint, but God never does. Is there no man who is what he says he is? Yes, and it is Jesus Christ Himself.

(I sometimes see the truth more clearly when I am unhappy. I wrote this after realizing a guy I was talking to all ready had a girlfriend. God reveals why things happen the way they do to protect me. That is the real love relationship.)

Obedience

I am struggling to maintain peace because my mom has been hospitalized for two weeks with the past five days in intensive care. Life threatening situations repeated themselves most recently yesterday and this morning. I go to the Bible for peace and comfort. It is here that I find rest in Him. A friend shared where they had read this morning in the word so I went there and God revealed to me some mighty things. 1 Kings 17:2-5 "Then the word of the Lord came to Elijah. Leave here, turn eastward and hide in the Kerith Ravine, east of the Jordan. You will drink from the brook, and I have ordered the ravens to feed you there. So he did what the Lord had told him." So he _did_ what the Lord had told him. Obedience. First, we must listen to receive the word from God and when we hear him we must obey God. God has plans for your provision all along with the crises in your life, but you must listen and obey. Verse 6 "The ravens brought him bread and meat in the morning and bread and meat in the evening, and he drank from the brook." I am understanding the symbolism for us here is to seek God's word (the bread) in the morning and evening and He will provide you with (the meat) things important for your sustenance in life through difficult times. You will then drink from (the brook) or the living waters God provides as a flowing source of nourishment in our lives through Him. Praise God for speaking to us through the word, His divine ability to teach us to listen and obey, and His provision of the living waters. You are an AMAZING GOD! By being obedient God has given me the strength and provision I need this morning to face this difficult time. He will do the same for you.

It is interesting how God uses some of these devotions to bless me as I am typing them for publication. They are pertinent for the situation I am facing at the time. I am in the middle of a family crisis now and I needed to receive this. I guess that is what it means by receiving a double portion. God doesn't waste anything. Amen?

People will draw to you for advice if they feel you have weathered a storm yourself. I'd have to say that is one of the greatest blessings of hardship is being able to be there for someone else to share the same love to them during a hurtful time that God shared with me. I found out my husband was having an affair seven years before our marriage ended. Obviously I took him back because we stayed together seven years longer. One of my dearest friends came to me and poured her heart out about the affair her husband was having. I listened and cried with her as we experienced her pain together. In desperation she asked me what she should do. God gave me the words to say as I told her to "love him more." She followed that advice and I am happy (somehow the word happy is just not enough) to say their marriage has survived and flourished. Romans 12:10 "Be devoted to one another in brotherly love. Honor one another above yourselves." If anything I have been through could guide someone else on their journey I pray that   1Timothy 4:12 I can "Set an example…. In speech, in life, in love, in faith and in purity." All the glory goes to God as His love in me spills over onto others. Please don't allow bitterness to spill over onto others but the positive, sweet spirit which allows you to "Love More."

No Smell of Smoke

It was time to clean up some old files and sentimental fool that I am I kept a whole file on love memories from my ex. Depending on where you are now in your divorce you may think this was harsh but I took the stack of love letters to an open space outside and burned them. My neighbor said, "Marian, what are you doing?" I said, "Burning my past." At that time my ex had married and I was moving on with my life.

The scripture I can find to relate to this is Hebrews 12:1 "Let us throw off everything that hinders and the sin that so easily entangles, and let us run with perseverance the race marked out for us." I recommend like the T.V. shows sometimes warn that you don't try this at home (burning the letters).. This was what worked best for me to close out one chapter of my life. I am focusing on Jesus as He shows me how to run the race marked out for me. Parts of my life may go up in smoke but like Shadrach, Meshack, and Abednego I am emerging with no hair on my head singed and no smell of smoke on me. I trust in Him to give me the perseverance to complete this race.

Liar, Liar

Lies, Lies, Lies about where you've been, who you've been with, where that money went. Lies told so convincingly that I even begin to believe them myself. Even worse the person telling the lies has told lies so often until they believe what they are saying to be true. Things I can't put my finger on but my gut feeling isn't good about those responses to my questions. I know in my heart they are lies but I can't prove it. Have I lured you in to condemnation of someone else because this has happened to you? That is where the second Liar in the title comes in. 1 John 1:8 "Any man who believes he has no sin deceives himself."

I am no better than this liar because I haven't been truthful with myself or with God about the deception in my heart. Yes, my sweet friend, it is difficult in life to learn that many times the lesson is about us and not pointing the finger at someone else. What have I done in my life that was wrong? John 1:5 "The light shines in the darkness, but the darkness has not understood it." Lord, let the light shine in the darkest parts of my heart where I have been untruthful with you and cause my heart to understand it. Break my judgment of others and focus my attention on truths about myself to give me the freedom you promised. Give me the gift of compassion and mercy to those who have been untruthful to me so that lies will become truths. Jesus said John 12:47 "For I did not come to judge the world but to save it." Thank you, Jesus, for not judging me. I will do better about learning to not judge others. For the truth about myself shall set me free. Amen.

So who is the liar you or me?

God is Love

How many times have you heard "God is Love?" Well, now the difference is it is time to put some power into those words to understand the meaning and significance of them. Now there is no one else to turn to. Your children aren't with you right now. Your spouse is gone because of a divorce you didn't ask for. Family and friends are tired of hearing about your situation. It is an afternoon or dark evening alone and it is time to dig deep. Everything is despair.

That is Satan and that is a lie. "God is close to the brokenhearted." Psalm 34:18. God hears your pleas for help. No one else answered, but God does. Jeremiah 31:3-4 "The Lord appeared to us in the past (and present) saying: 'I have loved you with an everlasting love; I have drawn you with loving-kindness. I will build you up again and you will be rebuilt." God says He loves with an EVERLASTING love. A love that never, never ends. God is loving you now with loving kindness. God will rebuild you and hold you up through the difficult times. My divorce counselor read to me Isaiah 54:5-6 "For your Maker is your husband-the Lord Almighty is his name-the Holy One of Israel is your Redeemer, he is called the God of all the earth. The Lord will call you back as if you were a wife deserted and distressed in spirit…" Allow God to call you back from the pit of despair to love on you. Spend time with Him.Give Him opportunities to show you what TRUE LOVE really is. A love who never abandons you. God is Love.

Exist in God

About a year ago I had leg surgery which required an overnight stay in the hospital. My sons came to take me home. While we were waiting for my release my oldest son's cell phone rang. I recognized his father's voice. In the course of the conversation my son told his dad he was at the hospital with his mom. No reply. Later that afternoon I asked my son what his dad (and my husband for 24 years) said in response to that. He said, "You know, Mom, it is as if you don't exist. He doesn't talk or ask about you at all." As hurtful as those words might sound God has brought me to such a place of security with my love that God has for me that He comforts me at all times. My prayer for you is for you to receive that comfort from Him and He will supply all your needs. He thinks of me more often than there are numbers of grains of sand in this entire world. He knows my wants and innermost needs in detail more than the countless galaxies of stars in the sky. He has a name for every star in the sky and He loves me more than that. He knew me when He created the heavens and the earth and even before I was formed in my mother's womb. Just as I recognized my ex-husband's voice on the phone I recognize God's voice as He speaks to me through scriptures of love, encouragement from friends, inspirational sermons, and natural beauty he reveals to me. My existence is in God. Thank you, Lord, for loving me like that.

Joy from the Mourning

In order to get to the mountaintop you must pass through the valleys. How can you appreciate the panoramic views from the wide open mountaintop if you haven't hiked through the limited distance vision in the valleys? Don't beat yourself up if you are in a valley of mourning right now. Just as there are stages of grief there are stages God passes us through of sorrow to get to joy. The scripture Psalm 30:5 "rejoicing comes in the morning" with a play on words that sound alike morning and mourning to: rejoicing comes from the mourning. It is okay to grieve and cry over a tremendous loss in your life. God wants to bless you with joy. Galatians 5:22 "Love, joy, peace, patience, kindness, goodness, faithfulness, gentleness and self-control." After all joy is the second fruit of the spirit. How do you pass from sorrow to joy? Psalm 119:28 "My soul is weary with sorrow; strengthen me according to your word." His word promises to fully redeem you even from sorrow. Psalm 145:13 "The Lord is faithful to all his promises and loving toward all he has made." Psalm 130:7 "O, Israel, put your hope in the Lord, for with the Lord is unfailing love and with him is full redemption." He is not going to partially redeem you from sorrow he is going to FULLY redeem you. Psalm 147:3-5 shows there is no doubt He is capable of doing that "He heals the brokenhearted and binds up their wounds. He determines the number of the stars and calls them each by name. Great is our Lord and mighty in power; his understanding has no limit." Comforting to know? Psalm 119:76 "May your unfailing love be my comfort, according to your promise to your servant." I can't stop finding scripture references to lead you to joy. Psalm 107:6 "Then they cried out to the Lord in their trouble, and he delivered them from their distress." God strengthens, promises, redeems, heals, understands, comforts, and delivers. What else do you need to know? "Light is shed upon the righteous and joy on the upright in heart." Psalm 97:11 Joy comes.

Trying Hard

During the last two years of my marriage I tried so hard to win my husband's love and affection back because I was receiving none. I truly took responsibility for the relationship plotting in my mind ways to be attractive enough, sexy enough, considerate enough... whatever it took to win him back. He was having an affair and I saw our marriage going down the tubes. It was becoming all -consuming so much so that my teenage sons told me later that I almost lost them during this time because the majority of my efforts were directed at my husband. The scripture I just read is perfect for this. Galatians 1:10 "Am I now trying to win the approval of men, or of God? Or am I trying to please men? If I were still trying to please men, I would not be a servant of Christ." Praise God for His love He lavished on me. All this time of rejection, difficulty and struggle where my husband and I lived together but were like two ships passing in the night, his passing me by unnoticed, God was drawing me closer to Him. I thought I could win my husband over. Nothing I could do in my power worked. Seeking to please man is not where I stand now. I am a "servant of Christ" and have released my man approval to God. I have redirected my focus to God and strive daily to seek Him first. This is a healthy prescription for relationships because Matthew 6:33 says "Seek ye first the kingdom of God and all these things will be added unto you." Quit trying to win man's approval and seek God instead. He will work out the other relationships in your best interest.

Life Lessons

It is amazing how God will use anything in our surroundings to be life lessons if we stay focused on him. I have received messages from Him most frequently in my quiet just "listening times" when I am outside looking at His beautiful creation or in everyday circumstances.

I have this beautiful tapestry form India I am very attached to. It is a huge piece and occupies a big expanse of wall. It is very unusual with pieces of costumes from India sewn together to make a beautiful display of threads and colors. My boys can't stand it. (Oh well, what do they know about not gaudy as opposed to good taste? Like they say "beauty is in the eyes of the beholder." Lol) Anyway this huge framed picture came crashing down and broke into hundreds of pieces of glass and broken frame on the floor. (I was just thankful it fell while I was out rather than during the night. I probably would have died of a heart attack-living alone, hearing a crash like that. I would have thought a burglar was breaking in!) Glass pieces were all over the room, on the table, on the chairs- you name it! It fell in July and with reframing time and finding someone to rehang it took six months to fix. The lesson in that is I appreciate it now more than I did before because I was without it so long and the reframing looks better than the original. The new frame is better and I didn't realize how dusty the tapestry had gotten. It looks cleaner and the colors are more vivid. What that reminds me of is what God has done with my life. What was once broken and shattered has been a mending process, he has done for me to make me better than I ever was before. What I didn't tell you was the reason the picture fell in the first place was wire that wasn't strong enough for the weight of the picture. I am thankful our faith in God is strong enough for us to see us through. Without our strong support in Christ our lives would come crashing down. Continue to trust God with the weight of your problems. Meanwhile, in the trial times look for God to send you messages in the smallest details of life as he did for me with this picture. Those are His love letters to you.

Love Prayer

I just found some scripture that is so reassuring. Hebrews 7:24-25 "….but because Jesus lives forever, he has a permanent priesthood. Therefore he is able to save completely those who come to God through him, because he always lives to intercede for them." Because he <u>always</u> lives to <u>intercede</u> for them. Christ hears our prayers of intercession and presents them to God the Father on our behalf. Isn't that amazing?

My favorite stained glass window is the scene of Jesus praying at Gethsamene. Seeing Jesus on his knees is the sweetest love image of Him I have. To think that He cares enough and loves me enough to pray for me and intercede on my behalf to God. This example of selfless love makes me want to be on my knees on behalf of my family, friends, and others. Have you ever heard anyone say, "I could feel your prayers?" Have you ever experienced strength that was unexplainable in trying times and later a friend said, "I was praying for you?"

This is how we make it day by day. Stop to think about your parents and grandparents who prayed for you daily. Not a one of those prayers was unheard and still those prayers are there for you today. Jesus loves us even more than our family members!   If I may have the liberty to change this scripture 1John 4:19 "We love because He first loved us" to we pray, because He first <u>prayed</u> for us. Prayer and love…Hum, could be those actions are synonymous.

Temptation Looks so Good
But Not God (I)

Satan knows what to tempt each of us with, and he knows how to make it look good. Loneliness comes with separation and divorce. I have dated time and time again but these relationships ended. Why? God is protecting me.

One relationship was the best one I had experienced. He said all the right things, did all the right things, except he kept pushing me to give something I didn't give. Only with God's help was I able to resist. We dated for a year.I felt God telling me to end this relationship, but I tried to ignore these messages. Surely I wouldn't have to give him up.

Finally, a devotion spoke directly to me. The scripture was 2 Samuel 11:1-5. The points made in the devotion were 1. verse 1 David was at the wrong place at the wrong time. He was supposed to be at battle with his men. 2. verse 2 David couldn't sleep. He was out on the roof looking at things of the world instead of looking to heaven and spending time with God. When you seek spiritual things you find God's guidance, grace, and mercy to help you through lonely or difficult times. Satan knew just how to tempt David. When you're in trouble or alone seek God.

Temptation Looks so Good
But Not God (2)

Point 3 verse 3-Heed the warning. David asks who the beautiful woman was bathing and the man warns him it is Bathsheba, the wife of Uriah. This was a clear warning because she was married, but David didn't heed the warning. I was receiving warnings to give up my relationship. He was divorced and so was I, but God was telling me to end the relationship. I wasn't heeding the warnings. 4. verse 4 David sent messengers to get her. She came to him and he slept with her. She became pregnant and matters only became worse. David had Uriah killed.

The lesson to be learned from this scripture was 1. being at the wrong place at the wrong time 2. not looking to Jesus and 3. not heeding the warning. I realized God was speaking directly to me through this and I ended the relationship.

We think we know what is best for us, but we don't. God does. In Genesis Eve was tempted to eat the fruit because it looked so good and it would give her wisdom. How often do we fall into temptation because it looks so good and we think we are so wise? Don't pay attention to Satan's temptations. Pray-Lord, lead us not into temptation, but deliver us from evil.

Temptation Looks so Good
But Not God (3)

I think I should change this title to deception looks so good but is not God. My spirit is very grieved as I write this. My entire being is sadness, disappointment, and dismay. I just got home from a church play where the characters showed examples of ungodly lives, certain groups of people were made the brunt of jokes that weren't funny, scriptures were used as jokes, sexual innuendoes were rampant, and bad examples of lifestyles were enacted on stage. All this was in a church play. I was convicted to leave because all of these things were being laughed at. People were laughing at things that weren't even funny. Worse than that the minister had written this play. Thank goodness my friend I was with was convicted to leave because I was ready to walk out myself. The doors of the church were locked down. Why were we locked in? All of this made us feel tremendously uncomfortable.

The thought that came to me was Jesus on the temple steps as he overturned the tables of the moneychangers. Have we so rejected Jesus until we can't recognize evil when we see it? John 12:40 says "He has blinded their eyes and deadened their hearts, so they can neither see with their eyes, nor understand with their hearts, nor turn-and I would heal them." Skipping to verse 42 "Yet at the same time many among the leaders believed in Jesus. But because of the Pharisees they would not confess their faith for fear they would be put out of the synagogue; for they loved praise from men more than praise from God." What have each of us participated in, agreed to and laughed at lightly when indeed it was not of God and a serious matter? Are we so swayed by our love of man's approval until we are afraid to stand up against the world and stand for what is right in God? God is calling us to be a light in a dark place where temptation looks so good but is not God. I pray God will open our eyes so that we can see God's power clearly and He will appear quickly with his healing touch. Then Satan's attempts will be bound and God will prevail.

John 12:35 "Walk while you have the light, before darkness overtakes you. The man who walks in the dark does not know where he is going. Put your trust in the light while you have it so that you may become sons of light." We are trusting in your light, Lord, to show us the way so that we will become those sons of light making a stand for what is right.

Grow

How could one little four- letter word be so powerful? The command God wants us to hear is "Grow." Jesus told the parable of the seed. Seed fell on rocky places and did not establish a root. Then another seed fell among thorns and was choked out. Finally, there was the seed that fell on good soil and produced large crops. Matthew 13:3-9. Grow as defined in Webster's Dictionary means "to come into being also to become attached or united by growth." I don't know about you but I understand that power is spoken in one little word- "Grow." I want to become attached to God and allow His work in me to unite me with Him in growth. Luke 2:52" Jesus grew in wisdom and stature, and in favor with God and men: The fact that Jesus grew is humbling. If Jesus needed to grow then what do I need to do? In Romans 8:14 "The true children of God are those who let God's Spirit lead them." Are we growing or stagnant like the pools of water with algae growing on them? Lord, I pray for each of us that our seed will fall on good soil and produce large crops for your Glory. "Grow" is such a small word but such a powerful part of our spiritual life. Lord, Bless our season of enrichment with Growth. Amen.

God's Temple

I am just going to be quite open and honest with you- having sexual intimacy in a marriage and then having it taken away from you is very difficult. Some single friends and I have talked about how this challenge to be pure is harder now than when we were in high school because we didn't know what we were missing then. God knows our struggles with this. 1 Corinthians 6:18-20 "Flee from sexual immorality. All other sins a man commits are outside his body, but he who sins sexually sins against his own body. Do you not know that your body is a temple of the Holy Spirit, who is in you, whom you have received from God? You are not your own; you were bought at a price. Therefore honor God with your body." It doesn't get more clear than that. The Holy Spirit lives in us and that is a temple for His dwelling. If God loved me enough to buy me at the price of sacrificing his only son on the cross to die for my benefit, then surely I can sacrifice sexual desires which is still for my benefit. The benefit is following God's plan for sex in a covenant relationship of marriage where there are commitments and not just pleasure for the moment and then abandonment. Here again the laws God sets forth are for our own protection and what is best for us. It hurts to get attached to someone physically and then have them leave you behind with those emotional and sexual soul ties. We have all experienced that. God intended a relationship for you of commitment and fulfillment. 1 Corinthians 7:5 "Then come together again (in a marriage) so that Satan will not tempt you because of your lack of self –control. " Pray for God to give you the self control you need so that you can honor God with your body. The benefit is keeping the Holy Spirit in you. I want the Holy Spirit to dwell in my temple and I anticipate sex again within marriage. Dwell in my temple, Lord!

Lead by example

The first family event I attended with my ex and his wife was tough. God gave me the strength to extend grace and mercy as I presented some of the photo albums to the new wife to keep for my ex to remember days gone by and for my sons. My children were watching the interaction between the two of us. I guess they wondered what in the world their mom was saying to the ex's new wife. They could tell by the expression on my face that it was not confrontational but with quietness and grace with which I presented a book of photos which was a treasure to me I was sharing with her. Romans 12:14 "Wish good for those who harm you; wish them well and do not curse them." God has led me to a point to pray for my ex in his marriage and even more difficult to pray was that his new wife would be a good mother to my boys. Years later I have witnessed the forgiveness my son has issued to his ex in a sadly similar scenario which has also ended his marriage. Perhaps the hurts I suffered were so that I could encourage my son through his difficult valley. I am so proud to hear him say he has forgiven his ex and wishes her happiness and contentment. John 8:12 "Jesus said I am the light of the world. Whoever follows me will never walk in darkness, but will have the light of life." No light to walk in at night? Are you stumbling in everyday events that come your way? Prayers aren't being answered? Attack after attack comes your way? Perhaps it is unforgiveness in your heart. Don't allow unforgiveness and Satan to have any footing in your life. Let the devil fall on his face in the dark. Allow Jesus to shine the light of a forgiving heart on you so that you will see clearly even in the darkest of nights because the light of life, Jesus will be with you. You never know when your actions are being observed by your children and it may impact their lives as well. John 12:36 "Put your trust in the light while you have it, so that you may become sons of light." I am putting my trust in the light so that my sons may <u>become</u> those sons of light. I pray their acts of forgiveness will shine light for someone else to see clearly some day. Lead by example so the ones you love most will benefit most.

1 John 3:21-22 "Dear friends, if our hearts do not condemn us, we have confidence before God and receive from him anything we ask, because we obey his commands and do what pleases Him." Having confidence in God allows our hearts to be in the right place and we don't feel condemned. Quit carrying around that baggage of "Oh, if only I had done this in our marriage" or "If only I had done that." God doesn't condemn us. That is of Satan. If we live our lives according to how God wants us to and keep His commandments, He will reward us with our desires. The confidence you have before God allows us to walk into a room of married couples even though we are alone. The confidence you have before God gives us the sense of security to go to a movie or restaurant alone and still have a smile on your face. The confidence we have before God allows us to share our testimony with others or to just be quiet and listen when someone else shares their pain with us. The confidence we have before God prevents us from saying negative things about our ex around our children even though the conversation was a perfect lead in to that. In doing all these things we please Him, our heart lifts, and joy becomes a part of who we are: as God leads us from condemnation to commendation. After all the only promotion worth having is from God!

Unity in the Community

I live on a small lake. I was watching three separate groups of geese in groups of
9-12 on the lake. Two new geese flew in and swam with their necks outstretched parallel to the water. I suppose that was a sign of subservience with bowed head and to show the others no harm was intended. The interesting thing was none of the existing groups welcomed them in and it is apparent to me the three groups all ready there did not mix. I found it strange that here they are the same kind of birds and they don't even welcome each other. It reminded me of us as churches or denominations which stay apart and sometimes provide an unwelcoming environment. John 10:14-16 "I am the good Shepherd; I know my sheep and my sheep know me-just as the Father knows me and I know the Father-and I lay down my life for the sheep. I have other sheep that are not of this sheep pen. I must bring them also. They too will listen to my voice, and there shall be one flock and one shepherd." Kind of humbling isn't it? Jesus says there will be sheep not from this pen that He would even lay his life down for when WE don't even welcome outsiders. I don't understand how we geese keep some out but I know community to be one flock under the ONE shepherd, Jesus Christ. We should follow His desires in wanting to bring us together as one flock.

Time Wasted or Not?

Acts 8:5 "Phillip went down to a city in Samaria and proclaimed the Christ there." God may take you out of a comfort zone of where Jesus is known to a place like Samaria where Jesus is not known. A Godly friend of mine asked me two years ago to accompany him to witness to a female. This middle-aged woman had been a pianist and organist for a small church but had stopped attending due to medical problems. No one from her church had come to visit her. As a result she was angry at God for her infirmities and at her congregation for the lack of love and outreach to her. She was racked with much pain when we got there and her countenance was dark. She hardly talked or responded to us at all. The husband's face showed his worry and concern for her. We sang and prayed with her but nothing seemed to work. I sang "He touched Me" (and believe me I am no great vocalist) but God put it on my heart to do that. We were only there for about twenty minutes. I left feeling discouraged because nothing I shared of encouragement regarding God being with me during and after my divorce and about God being with me in a dark time seemed to work. Was it time wasted? Did I not say the right things?

Two years later I received a call from the same friend who shared the glorious news that this lady had rededicated her life to Christ and she wanted to see me. To see me? Wow was I humbled. We tried on several different days to go see her, but our schedules didn't mesh. The next call I got was my friend calling to say the lady had been to the doctor and been diagnosed with a tumor on her brain. She wanted my friend and me to meet her at the neurologist's office to talk and pray with her. Again I was humbled by the request. We went and even though I had only met her once I immediately recognized her in the crowded waiting room.

My friend and I talked with words of encouragement. She stood and gave me a hug and demonstrated to me how she could even walk which she was not able to do before. More amazing than that was the difference in her appearance. Where she had been dark and sullen before she was now bright in complexion and radiant. She virtually glowed when she smiled and she spoke so freely to us now about her love for Christ. Oh, I could see the difference in the husband's relieved expressions as well. They looked at each other often with that loving, knowing look which partners share. It was an amazing transformation. She spoke as though Jesus may not leave her here long, but we spoke words of healing over her. This friend and I kneeled and prayed with her right there in the crowded waiting room lobby. This time my friend sang for her. I sensed that everyone in that lobby knew the seriousness of the timing of our visit. We prayed for the doctors, nurses, and Jesus's plan for her life and praised God for her renewal of faith. She told me she had even begun to play the piano again and I told her the angels were rejoicing in heaven over that.

I don't know what Samaria God is calling you to but I can tell you from experience being obedient and going there even if it is out of your comfort zone is well worth it. You will experience a joy indescribable. Who knows what other lives were touched that day in the crowded waiting room? On our way out a lady grabbed my arm and said, "Blessings on you sweet sister in Christ." My friend and I both spoke a blessing over her in return. All it took was a twenty minute visit to a lady in a dark time. Time wasted or not? It was a God ordained visit which impacted an eternity. Be obedient and make the trip to Samaria. God is good in His timing and ALL THE TIME!

How Deep and Wide
Is a Mother's Love?

In the Intensive Care Unit for my mom I picked up her Bible to read in Romans and opened directly to Chapter 5. I wept openly with a rush of emotion as I saw she had handwritten on Dec. 31, 2003 "Hope for Marian and husband's healing for marriage." Wow! How deep and wide is a Mother's love? All I could think about was Ephesians 3:17-18 "And I pray that you being rooted and established in love may have power, together with all the saints to grasp how wide and long and high and deep is the love of Christ…" My mother exemplified this Christlike love for me by praying for my marriage. This entry was put in her Bible just four days after my husband left. I can just see her tears of anguish over our failed marriage. She was seeking hope, courage, and support in God's word. How wide and long and high and deep is the love of a mother's heart created by God to love like He does? Nothing brings me sweeter reassurance at this time than to know my mother loved me and my husband that much to write in her Bible the hope she had for us came from the deep love of Christ in her. God eased her pain and anguish over our divorce. In Romans 5:1 "In happy certainty of the glorious things He has for us in the future." (J.B. Phillips translation) My future turned out well from the time she wrote this and I'm certain your future is going to turn out even better, Mom. That is how wide and long and high and deep God's love is for you.

God's Will to be Done

I am sitting in the ICU at the hospital looking at my mother who is hooked up to a ventilator and so sedated she is unaware of all the hoses and life support lines in her body. She is in a coma. This morning the nurses acted quickly to save her life. Her condition is stable and it is a matter of waiting for tests to determine what is best for her future. The doctor says she will either have the will to live or she won't. I am encouraged by listening to the soothing sound of the oxygen pump as the oxygen flows to her lungs, and I am trusting in God for His will to be done.

I opened a book on <u>Prayer</u> by Charles Spurgeon and you'll never guess what I opened to. "Your will be done." Matthew 6:10 "Your will be done on earth as it is in heaven." My mind is blessed with comforting thoughts of heaven where God's will <u>IS DONE</u>. Can you imagine how wonderful heaven is that all that is accomplished is God's will? That is what sets it apart in the heavenlies from the earth. Only God's will is done-Only good, no evil, Only joy, no sorrow. God's presence. Walking with Jesus and all those saints who have gone before us would be wonderful. Yesterday in delirium she said aloud the garden she saw was more beautiful than any she had ever seen with such new plants. Maybe she was catching a glimpse then of heaven. My glimpse is the comfort in His word that God's Will is Done in heaven. Allow us to see heaven on earth clearly when we do God's will on earth because one day eternity will be our blessing with God's will every day forever.

(Mom spent 4 days in the coma and a total of one month in the hospital. We received word that 100 missionary friends were praying for her. She did a complete turnaround and attended a national missionary board meeting she was in charge of at her church one month later. She is also feeling better and more active than she ever was before the illness. God has blessed us with allowing us to have her a little while longer. Who knows maybe even a lot longer! Her pastor said, "God just isn't through with you yet, Miss Anne.) I pray He isn't through with us yet either.

The other night I was lying on my back on the dock looking up at a wide, open, beautiful expanse of starry sky. I asked the Lord to please show me a falling star. The soft reply in my head was, "Not yet, my child. Not yet."

How many times in your life has God given you that answer, Not yet? A buddy of mine and I laugh because God keeps telling us to wait over and over. We smile and say thank you for that confirmation. We get it! We get it! (God probably says then why do you keep asking for it?) Isaiah 49:23… "Those who wait for the Lord shall renew their strength. They shall mount up with the wings of eagles, they shall run and not grow weary, they shall walk and not faint."
Isaiah 49:23 … "Those who hope in me will not be disappointed." How about those who wait in me will not be disappointed? God knows every minute detail of our life. Everything that we want in life is right now, but God knows what is best for us. In Acts Chapter one Jesus said 1:4 "But wait… For the gift my Father promised…"
God has many gifts He wants to give us. As He said in Isaiah hope in me, wait in me. How about the gift of Him in us that allows us to wait in Jesus? What He can give you now is the gift of the Holy Spirit in you to give you the strength you need to handle the delay to things you most want while he completes you. "Not yet, my child. Not yet."

*Many months after I wrote this I did get to see the most beautiful falling comet I had ever seen. I was in the darkness of my apartment praying face down on the floor praying about some serious issues in my family's life. I sat up, looked out the window and the sky was full of stars. About that time a huge comet went flaring through the sky like a big ball of fire with a tail attached. The bright white of the star was also changing colors of red, blue, and green. It was incredibly beautiful. It fell for what seemed minutes but I know it was only seconds. Had God not gotten me up off the floor to admire the beauty of the night sky I would have missed my blessing. He was saving it for now. Now my child. Now.

Realize the end
Or was it the beginning?

Realize the end of something and move on. The end may be leading you to another beginning. Just like the end of this devotion book I sense the Lord telling me to end it and finish the task. (Actually it hasn't been a task it has been a blessing.) When I was a little girl in first grade I wrote some books with my incorrect spelling, told a story, and even illustrated the book. In third grade I wrote a short story and it was published in the small town local newspaper. To earn extra money I wrote a one page newspaper by collecting news worthy of print from neighbors who were trying to relax on their front porch. I bombarded them with questions which they so happily answered for me. Exciting news was who was in town for a visit, who was sick, who was on vacation, and even an ad column to sell items. All this valuable information and I sold the paper for ten cents a copy. God planted a seed a long time ago. I would love to hear your story of how you can look back and see the stepping stones to get to where you are now. Realize that God equips you all through your life for what He has planned for you. Jeremiah 2:11 "For I know the plans I have for you, declares the Lord, plans to prosper you and not to harm you, plans to give you hope and a future." I pray that you will walk in the fullness of God as He reveals knowledge of the truth to you about your purpose. Realize when to start the walk and when to finish the walk. As some things conclude others begin. You may be embarking on a new journey God has led you to your entire life. Maybe even maybe it was necessary for some doors to close for you to get there.

I have no clue what is next but I anticipate this walk with Christ one day at a time.

Conclusion

Therefore, "They are before the throne of God
And serve him day and night in his temple;
And he who sits on the throne will spread his tent over them.
Never again will they hunger;
Never again will they thirst.
The sun will not beat upon them,
Nor any scorching heat.
For the Lamb at the center of the throne will be their shepherd;
He will lead them to springs of living water.
And God will wipe away every tear from their eyes."

Revelation 7:15-17